The Writing on the Wall

Also by Maggi Dawn
The Accidental Pilgrim

MAGGI DAWN

The Writing on the Wall

HODDER

Unless indicated otherwise, Scripture quotations are taken from the
Holy Bible, Today's New International Version.
Copyright © 2004 by International Bible Society.
Used by permission. All rights reserved.

First published in Great Britain in 2010 by Hodder & Stoughton
An Hachette UK company
This paperback edition published in 2012

1

Copyright © Maggi Dawn, 2010

A CIP catalogue record for this title is available from the British Library

ISBN 978 0 340 98004 0
Ebook ISBN 978 1 444 72207 9

Printed and bound by CPI Group (UK) Ltd, Croydon, CR0 4YY

Hodder & Stoughton policy is to use papers that are natural, renewable
and recyclable products and made from wood grown in sustainable forests.
The logging and manufacturing processes are expected to conform to the
environmental regulations of the country of origin.

Hodder & Stoughton Ltd
338 Euston Road
London NW1 3BH

www.hodderfaith.com

Contents

Preface

The Bible tells the story of the human race, beginning in a garden and ending in a city. In between it is full of ancient history, good advice, deep spirituality, morality tales, poetry, theology and even a few jokes. Its stories are not laid out chronologically, and it is the work of so many different authors, in different genres and from different times, that although it seems like a book it would be more apt to call it a small library. By turns it is outrageous and deeply comforting, and while some of it is strangely incomprehensible, other parts read as if it were written only yesterday.

The Bible is, of course, principally a religious book. But because of its central place in two millennia of Western culture, its language and imagery find echoes in art, music and literature wherever we look.

Samuel Taylor Coleridge, in his *Table Talk*, said that 'intense study of the Bible will keep any writer from being vulgar in point of style'.[1] Countless writers, artists and musicians down the centuries steeped themselves in the rhythms and imagery of the Bible until – almost unconsciously – it spilled over into their own language. And equally the ideas and insights of their work were read back into the pages of Scripture.

The Bible is much more, then, than a book for religious readers. It has been one of the main building blocks of our culture, and to leave it unread is to lose thousands of inferences and allusions, and to lose layers of meaning in everything else we read. But people no longer grow up with a background knowledge of the Bible that earlier generations could presume upon, and the complexity of its structure and the unfamiliarity of its contents mean that the Bible does not give up its secrets easily. Not only that, but like any great work it has many layers of meaning that are open to interpretation. What the Bible meant in Chaucer's time was not at all the same as what it meant for Fra Angelico, Handel or John Steinbeck.

The inspiration for this book came from hundreds of conversations with students at the University of Cambridge who, in the course of reading various Arts subjects, have knocked on my door to ask what the significance of this or that biblical or theological allusion might be: who is the King of Glory in the *Messiah*, why do the characters in *Hamlet* suffer such anxieties over death and hell, why does Jesus' mother often wear a crown, and who were the cheesemakers?

My aim here has been to sketch out the main themes and characters of the Bible, roughly in order, and to show some examples of how they have been interpreted in different centuries. This is merely a brief glimpse into subject matter that would need a whole library of books to begin to cover it well. Nevertheless, I hope that these chapters will open a window on the Bible, which is by turns exciting, shocking, inspiring, strange and comical, sometimes incomprehensible, but overall completely rewarding. And I hope that it might give a few leads to students of the future who are trying to figure out the origin and significance of phrases like 'Measure for Measure', 'East of Eden', 'Annunciation', or '*Nunc Dimittis*'.

To all the students who knocked on my door with their questions I offer thanks for many happy hours of conversation, and for inspiring me to write some of it down. I owe an even greater debt of thanks to Katherine Venn for commissioning and editing it, and to Ruth Roff, Wendy Grisham and all at Hodder who have helped bring it to birth. My thanks also to the many friends and colleagues who have generously given me advice and comments on various drafts, and especially to Luke Aylward, Jeremy Begbie, Sarah Dylan Breuer, Irving Finkel, Paul Fromont, Paula Gooder, Paul Judson, Robin Kirkpatrick, Rosalind Love, Henry Martin, Susan Sellers, Janet Soskice, Stephen Sykes, Jeremy Thurlow, Danielle Tumminio and Judy Weiss. Any errors are, of course, my own.

As always, I owe thanks to my son Ben for his help and patience as I have worked on this project. And I dedicate the book to the memory of my stepmother Pauline, who shared my love of the Bible and would have loved to see this book finished.

1

In the Beginning

On Christmas Eve 1968 Apollo 8, the first manned mission to the moon, entered lunar orbit. For the first time the earth was viewed from space, and the crew observed that it was the only planet that appeared to have any colour. Later that evening the voices of Commander Frank Borman, Command Module Pilot Jim Lovell and Lunar Module Pilot William Anders were heard on a live broadcast. 'The vast loneliness is awe-inspiring,' Lovell said, 'and it makes you realise just what you have back there on earth.' Then, capturing the traditional associations between creation, religion and Christmas, and expressing something of their own sense of wonder, the three astronauts ended their broadcast by reading from the first page of the King James Version of the Bible:

> In the beginning God created the heaven and the earth. And the earth was without form, and void; and darkness was upon the face of the deep. And the Spirit of God moved upon the face of the waters. And God said, Let there be light: and there was light.

> And God saw the light, that it was good: and God divided the light from the darkness. And God called the light Day, and the darkness he called Night. And the evening and the morning were the first day.
>
> And God said, Let there be a firmament in the midst of the waters, and let it divide the waters from the waters. And God made the firmament, and divided the waters which were under the firmament from the waters which were above the firmament: and it was so. And God called the firmament Heaven. And the evening and the morning were the second day.
>
> And God said, Let the waters under the heaven be gathered together unto one place, and let the dry land appear: and it was so. And God called the dry land Earth; and the gathering together of the waters called he Seas: and God saw that it was good.
>
> (Gen. 1:1–10 KJV)

The King James Bible, published in 1611, was translated into English by a whole committee of people, although much of it was drawn from the earlier work of William Tyndale (c. 1494–1536), who was the first person to translate the New Testament into English directly from the Greek and Hebrew. But the Bible itself is an amalgamation of a large number of texts of very ancient origin. Many of its stories are thought to date back to more than a thousand years BC, passed on in the oral traditions of various neighbouring tribes until they were eventually written down. It is thought that some more material was added in the seventh century BC by writers known as the Deuteronomists. Then in the sixth century BC

Jerusalem was overthrown and many of the Jews were taken into exile in Babylon. Far from their homeland, they sought to preserve their own national and religious identity, and so it was that they began to amalgamate and edit the various different traditions into one narrative, a task that continued when they eventually returned home.[1] The opening pages of Genesis, then, are thousands of years old. You might think that three men on the cutting edge of scientific development in the 1960s would find this ancient cosmology somewhat out of date. Why, in an age where science is king, would they include Genesis in their commentary as they emerged from their lunar orbit?

The answer to that question lies in understanding what kind of writing Genesis is. If one reads it with the assumption that it is a kind of primitive version of science that has long been disproved, then at best it will seem quaint. But Genesis is neither history (in the modern sense) nor primitive science: it is narrative literature written in poetic prose. Knowing what kind of literature you are reading completely affects what you expect it to tell you. The eminent physicist John Polkinghorne wrote:

> Mistaking poetry for prose can lead to false conclusions. When Robert Burns tells us his love 'is like a red, red rose', we know that we are not meant to think that his girlfriend has green leaves and prickles. Reading Genesis 1 as if it were a divinely dictated scientific text, intended to save us the trouble of actually doing science, is to make a similar kind of error.[2]

3

What kind of book is Genesis, then? It is listed in the Bible's contents page as the first of five books of 'the Law' – not law in the modern sense, but written to give shape and order to the whole understanding of life. These law books include some history, some biography, some theology and some legal and contractual material. And right at the beginning of Genesis there are eleven chapters of aetiology – a retrospective account of origins in terms of human purpose. That is to say, they are addressing the big questions about the human condition. What does it mean to be human? Why do we expect life to get better and not worse? Why do we fail ourselves and each other, and how is failure redeemed? What is our responsibility and relationship towards each other and towards the world in which we live? Why do we carry a kind of Utopian ideal in our head, even though we find ourselves consistently unable to achieve it? This discrepancy between the mythical possibility of a perfect universe and the imperfect reality of our world is what the ancient storytellers, and later the compilers, editors and translators of Genesis, were trying to frame with their account. In an aetiology, the question 'Where do we come from?' is not merely a question of a scientific description of how atoms and molecules behave, but a question of purpose – not so much how we got here, but why.

The King James Version of the Bible is hard to beat for the beauty of its seventeenth-century language. But while 'in the beginning' has commonly been taken to mean that God created something out of nothing, the Hebrew word could equally suggest that creation was concerned with bringing order out of a pre-existing chaos of matter – an idea that is echoed in another creation poem that appears in Isaiah

40:12–26. The creation myth, then, is a lot more fluid than it first appears and, far from being an alternative, anti-scientific cosmology, it is an ancient religious account of why there is both order and purpose to the human race.

Interestingly enough, the idea that Genesis should be taken as science is a relatively recent view. Long before the development of modern science, philosophers and theologians were treating the creation myths as metaphorical. There are examples of this even within the Bible itself. John's Gospel, written in the first or early second century AD, echoes the language of Genesis, and he expects his readers to make that connection and understand the gospel of Jesus Christ as a new beginning:

> In the beginning God created the heavens and the earth. Now the earth was formless and empty, darkness was over the surface of the deep, and the Spirit of God was hovering over the waters.
>
> And God said, 'Let there be light,' and there was light. God saw that the light was good, and he separated the light from the darkness.
>
> (Gen. 1:1–4)

> In the beginning was the Word, and the Word was with God, and the Word was God. He was with God in the beginning. Through him all things were made; without him nothing was made that has been made. In him was life, and that life was the light of all people. The light shines in the darkness, and the darkness has not overcome it.
>
> (John 1:1–5)

John takes the opening words, 'In the beginning . . .' to signal that the gospel marks a new beginning, a new ordering of creation under God. Similarly, he echoes from Genesis the first words of God, 'Let there be light', and shapes his Gospel around the contrast between darkness and light as a metaphor for the absence or presence of God – the new era of redemption through Christ being like a second genesis.

In the early centuries of Christianity, Genesis continued to be a foundational theme for writers. One example is St Augustine, one of the most influential writers in Western theology. His *Confessions*, written in about AD 398, has become a classic text in literature as well as theology, and it includes an account of how he converted to Christianity from a sect known as the Manichees who, rather than believing in the supremacy of a good God, believed that equal powers of good and evil were in a constant battle. Augustine was anxious to be absolutely clear that he had renounced their beliefs, and since his conversion believed in God as supreme and as the source of everything. In Books XII and XIII of *Confessions* he takes an allegorical view of Genesis, which was a popular practice of the time (in fact, it was considered heretical by some of Augustine's contemporaries to take a literal view of a six-day creation). He wrote another work entitled *The Literal Meaning of Genesis* (*De Genesi ad Litteram*), an in-depth, phrase-by-phrase analysis of the text that drew out the theological meaning of Genesis. But there was not a shred of young-earth creationism in it – in fact, quite the opposite. One of his stated intentions was to counter the simplistic interpretation of Genesis as science that – even in the fourth century – was so obviously mistaken as to bring Christianity into disrepute and make the Bible look like nothing more than a book of children's stories.

> It's shameful and dangerous for an unbeliever to hear a Christian talking nonsense about the Holy Scripture, and to assume that its meaning is being explained. We should make every effort to prevent the embarrassing situation where Christians are shown to be ignorant, and laughed to scorn – not that it matters if an ignorant person is ridiculed, but it's shameful if people outside the Church come to think that these were the opinions of the sacred writers.[3]

The language and themes of the creation stories have continued to echo through literature in every century since. One of the most famous literary meditations on Genesis is *Paradise Lost*. John Milton's aim was to retell the story of creation and the fall. His project, though, was not simply to elaborate imaginatively on the Genesis story, but to draw out political as well as theological interpretations. The work encompasses several different genres, but is usually described as an epic poem. The difficulty with calling it an epic, however, is that it is not really clear who the hero is, for while this is usually assumed to be Adam, you could just as easily read it taking Satan in the hero's role. Nonetheless, the main thrust of the poem is not really the destiny or identity of the hero, but the theme of freedom – in both the theological and the political sense – and even the form of the poem embodies this, for Milton seems quite deliberately to have illustrated the idea of freedom by writing in blank verse. Epic poems were always written in rhyming verse, but in a 'Note on the Verse' in the

1668 edition of *Paradise Lost*, Milton explained his choice of unrhyming blank verse as a recovery of 'ancient liberty' from the 'troublesome and modern bondage of Riming'.

Theologian Stephen Sykes has pointed out that to retell the biblical narrative in epic form limits its theological possibilities, because the epic form is focused on the hero, while theology has to be multidirectional. But the limitations of any literary form are also precisely what lend that form its power, and Milton both echoes and expands the language of Genesis in his magisterial and poetic description of creation:

> [I]n his hand
> He took the golden compasses, prepared
> In God's eternal store, to circumscribe
> This universe, and all created things . . .
>
> This God the Heav'n created, thus the earth,
> Matter unformed and void. Darkness profound
> Covered th'abyss; but on the wat'ry calm
> His brooding wings the Spirit of God outspread . . .[4]

A couple of centuries later, Gerard Manley Hopkins (1844–89) adopted the image of 'brooding wings' for the Holy Spirit, but for Hopkins there was a different purpose. 'The world is charged with the grandeur of God,' he wrote, and went on to show that God's creative energy was not isolated in an act of creation in the distant past, but was a continuing, nurturing power in the present age. Hopkins, though, was writing late in the nineteenth century when Christian thinking had cut itself loose from the idea that every movement of the earth was literally controlled by God. Like other poets and theologians of his age, he struggled to make sense of his belief that God was involved in the world, while also acknowledging that the earth had its own untamed chaos. The age-old question of why bad things happen to good people troubled Hopkins deeply, but he resolved it to some degree by understanding the presence of the Holy Spirit in creation not so much as an imposition of the power of God, but as a constant weaving and reweaving of creativity and human hope in a turbulent world. 'Nature is never spent,' wrote Hopkins, despite generations of death and destruction and despair:

> Because the Holy Ghost over the bent
> World broods with warm breast and with ah! bright
> wings.[5]

The rhythmic patterns of the language of Genesis 1 make it a natural hunting ground for poets, but not necessarily because they admire the sentiments. T.S. Eliot, for instance, adopts a series of phrases from the creation stories in *Choruses from 'The Rock' (VII)*, using his characteristic technique of percussive, almost rap-like repetition, to create a contemporary meditation on human purpose. But others have used the phraseology to subvert rather than reinforce Christian tradition, such as D.H. Lawrence who, in various poems, such as 'Let there be Light' and 'God is Born', reversed the sense of the biblical language to indicate that God was as much the product of evolution as everything else.

In the poetry of Genesis, Adam and Eve are presented as the first human couple, but read carefully and you will find not just one, but two accounts of their creation. Genesis begins with a list of all the things that were created, almost as if the writer is making a painting of the scene. It starts with the background – the heavens and the earth – and then the earth is added, and the sea, then trees and plants, the sun, moon and stars, all kinds of birds and fish and animals, and last of all the human race, a man and a woman both made at the same time. This first telling of the story places the human race as the kings-of-the-earth, the crowning glory of the whole enterprise, and the ones who become responsible for looking after it (quite the opposite, incidentally, of the Australian Aboriginal tradition where the people belong to the earth).

The creation of Adam and Eve is then retold in the second chapter, but this time the sequence is reversed. Instead of building up the background layer by layer, Genesis 2 starts with God creating a man – just one man. *Adam* is the Hebrew word for 'man' – the generic name for a human being – and it is similar, in Hebrew, to the word for 'earth', reflecting the idea that we are made of the very stuff of the earth. Scientists tell us that we are made of carbon – stardust; centuries earlier, it seems that by poetic and human instinct there was the knowledge that we and our universe are made of the same substance. God put Adam into a garden he had made earlier – the garden of Eden.

Paradise is a Persian word that literally means 'a walled garden', and the name *Eden* means the 'garden of delights'. It is no mistake that the title of the fantastic triptych by Heironymus Bosch (Madrid) is 'the garden of earthly delights' – a phrase that has since been used over and over again about beautiful and unusual gardens. An interview with author and cook Nigel Slater appeared in the *Daily Telegraph* under the title 'A Garden of Earthly Delights', which entertainingly quoted Slater as saying that the very first thing he planted in his own garden was an apple tree.

God, we are told in Genesis, introduced Adam one by one to all the creatures in the garden of Eden, but Adam found none of them to be a suitable companion for him. What he needed was someone who was both the same and yet different, someone who seemed to share the very essence of himself. This is where the spare-rib story comes from:

> So the LORD[6] God caused the man to fall into a deep sleep; and while he was sleeping, he took one of the man's ribs and then closed up the place with flesh. Then the LORD God made a woman from the rib he had taken out of the man, and he brought her to the man.
>
> The man said,
> 'This is now bone of my bones
> and flesh of my flesh;
> she shall be called "woman",
> for she was taken out of man.'
>
> (Gen. 2:21–3)

There are some exquisite Byzantine and medieval illuminations of Eve being drawn out of Adam's side, giving the appearance of two bodies with one pair of legs – for instance, *Creation of Eve* (Ecole Anglaise thirteenth century), Musée Marmotten, France. The Hebrew word translated as 'rib' is *tsela'*, which can mean 'side', 'chamber', 'rib' or 'beam'. Feminist theologians have pointed out that the traditional reading of 'rib' has been used to sublimate women, and the better translation would be 'side', supporting the idea that woman is man's equal and not his subordinate. This did not stop feminists using the phrase with irony, though. In the 1960s and 1970s in the UK, newsagents contained shelves of women's magazines which offered little more than recipes, knitting patterns, romantic stories and advice on domestic management. The backlash against this insistence upon women as domestic goddesses came in the form of a feminist magazine first published in the UK in 1972. Its title was *Spare Rib*.[7]

⇁

If the first creation account detailed the whole universe as being built layer upon layer, then the second version was an account of why people need each other. It is often said that people in love have an uncanny sense of recognition – the feeling that despite being completely different and in many ways unknown, you have known that person for ever. This seems to be Adam's reaction when he sets eyes on the woman for the first time, poetically expressed as 'bone of my bones and flesh of my flesh'. The imagery of a perfect partnership in a perfectly ordered garden of Eden is borrowed by Peter Redgrove in his poem 'Intimate Supper', which begins with all the elements of the creation story reinvented in a modern apartment – the light is electric, the firmament is his ceiling, the moving breath of the Spirit is his new hoover and the flowing water is his bath. The man, in beautiful surroundings in the cool of the evening, is at peace with himself and his God. But the poem ends poignantly, suggesting that even in the modern-day Eden of a perfectly ordered life people still do not want to be alone. The need for a mate described in a Bronze Age tale and recast by the Babylonian Jewish scholars seven centuries before Christ is a deep-seated human need that has lasted through centuries of cultural and religious change and adaptation:

> But the good sight faded
> For there was no help, no help meet for him at all,
> And he set his table with two stars pointed on wax
> And until the time came that he had appointed
> Walked in his garden in the cool of the evening,
>   waited.[8]

It is three decades since the astronauts on Apollo 8 quoted from the Bible to describe the dramatic beauty of the earth from space. Since then some pretty vociferous arguments have ensued as to the seeming clash between religious and scientific accounts of our origins. But the beauty of the Genesis account is precisely that it is an example of the human instinct to step beyond the cold facts and tell ourselves stories not only about how we are here, but why. That, I believe, is why it continues to be a rich source of inspiration for artists and poets, and one reason why, as they emerged from the dark side of the moon, Borman, Lovell and Anders chose the poetry of Genesis to express their celebration of wonder and their affirmation that the earth was good.

2
And all was for an apple

The British Museum was founded in 1753 when Sir Hans Sloane left his large collection of books, manuscripts, natural history specimens and antiquities to the nation. Among his collection was a manuscript containing this medieval carol:

> Adam lay ybounden
> Bounden in a bond:
> Four thousand winter
> Thought he not too long
>
> And all was for an apple,
> An apple that he took,
> As Clerkes finden
> Written in their book.

The words were used by Benjamin Britten in his intense and energetic 'Deo Gracias' (in *A Ceremony of Carols*), while a gentler and more lyrical version by Boris Ord is often featured in the Festival of Nine Lessons and Carols broadcast from King's College, Cambridge, on Christmas Eve. The words probably date from the fifteenth century, as the language places it as later than Chaucer but earlier than Shakespeare. 'And all was for an apple. . .' This one phrase summons up the central image of the Bible's account of where sin and suffering came from, and how a perfect universe became a lost paradise:

> The LORD God took the man and put him in the Garden of Eden to work it and take care of it. And the LORD God commanded the man, 'You are free to eat from any tree in the garden; but you must not eat from the tree of the knowledge of good and evil, for when you eat of it you will certainly die.'
>
> (Gen. 2:15–17)

Later, though, the snake in the grass whispered in Eve's ear, convincing her that God had been trying to trick her:

> Now the serpent was more crafty than any of the wild animals the LORD God had made. He said to the woman, 'Did God really say, "You must not eat from any tree in the garden"?'
>
> The woman said to the serpent, 'We may eat fruit from the trees in the garden, but God did say, "You must not eat fruit from the tree that is in the middle of the garden, and you must not touch it, or you will die."'
>
> 'You will not certainly die,' the serpent said to the woman. 'For God knows that when you eat of it your eyes will be opened, and you will be like God, knowing good and evil.'

When the woman saw that the fruit of the tree was good for food and pleasing to the eye, and also desirable for gaining wisdom, she took some and ate it. She also gave some to her husband, who was with her, and he ate it. Then the eyes of both of them were opened, and they realized they were naked; so they sewed fig leaves together and made coverings for themselves.

(Gen. 3:1–7)

Snakes are fascinating creatures. In the ancient world they were feared because of their capacity to kill by crushing or with deadly venom, but they were also revered because of their ability to shed their old skins and – apparently – be reborn. In equal measure they were worshipped as symbols of life and fertility and feared as agents of deception, evil and destruction.

In the Jewish and Christian traditions, the serpent that appears in Genesis is pure evil, a deceiver who subtly twists God's words to trick Eve into falling into her own destruction. Elsewhere in the Bible, the serpent is seen as sinister, associated with the primal chaos of the sea and the underworld. Revelation 12:9 refers to 'that ancient snake' which the Christian tradition has usually taken to be the devil or Satan, the enemy of God. But in the Ancient Near East, including Egypt and Canaan, and also in the Greco-Roman mythology that was prevalent in the cultures in which Christianity was born, the serpent was a symbol of fertility. It is not surprising, therefore, that the interpretation of the Genesis stories seems to include contradictions – so that while fertility and the need for a soulmate are recognised as good, sex is also regarded as sinful and forbidden.

The association between temptation and seduction in the creation stories appears frequently in Western medieval art, one example being a sculpture on the front of Notre Dame in Paris, in which a long serpent with a woman's face is wound round a tree. Another glamorous serpent-woman clutching golden apples is seen in conversation with Adam and Eve on a painted roof boss in Norwich Cathedral.

Seeing and perceiving is another prominent theme in the fall. The snake promised Eve that eating the fruit would open her eyes so that she would be like God. The eyes were also the portal of temptation, for she 'saw' that the fruit was good and 'pleasing to the eye', and finally it says that, indeed, their eyes were opened – but rather than being like God, they saw themselves and each other differently. Their perfect trust and intimacy were disrupted, and their unspoilt paradise infected with secrets and lies, shame and cover-ups.

We often use the word 'temptation' to describe harmless and trivial treats like eating chocolate. But while the piece of fruit that Adam and Eve ate was equally harmless in itself, the temptation lay in what it represented. The fruit was 'good to eat, and pleasing to the eye', but the sin lay in ignoring God's express wishes. The perfect harmony of Eden was broken, which led to alienation between Adam and Eve, and between them and God.

It has fairly consistently been agreed in the Christian tradition that pride – wanting to be godlike – was the underlying root of the problem. But both the fruit in the garden and the kind of surface temptation it represented have varied quite a lot. Genesis does not say what kind of fruit Adam and Eve ate, and paintings from different regions vary in their interpretation. The Mediterranean tradition tended towards figs, not only because they were a common fruit, but because Adam and Eve made their first clothes from fig leaves. In England the apple may simply have been the obvious choice because it was the most common local fruit, but it may have caught on because the same Latin word, *malum*, can mean either apple or evil.

As far as the temptation itself is concerned, it seems quite firmly lodged in the popular imagination that the temptation was sex. But in most writing and painting about the subject, this does not bear out. Augustine often associated sin with sex, and was renowned for his own struggles with sexual temptation. But as the main early theologian who articulated the idea of original sin – the idea that after the fall every human being was born sinful, not innocent – it is interesting to notice that to illustrate his point Augustine used a different allusion altogether. In his *Confessions* (Book II) he describes another story of fruit trees – not apples in this case, but pears – in which he joined a group of boys who went scrumping fruit in a nearby garden. Like Eve's temptation, you could say, 'It was only a piece of fruit!' But following the pattern of Genesis, Augustine looks under the surface of a relatively insignificant action to see what the deeper motive was, and then knocks down every excuse for this piece of childish mischief. He will not excuse himself by saying that he was young, or that he did not know any better, that others led him on, or that it was a relatively harmless act. He is clear that the sin is not defined by the act itself, but by a desire simply to rebel against accepted values, to break the rules just for the hell of it. By all accounts Augustine led a pretty colourful life, and had he wanted to he could easily have chosen a more sensational example of sin, or a more obviously destructive one. Perhaps he chose a relatively innocent anecdote to avoid creating a book that people would read salaciously. But I think it is more likely that he wanted to emphasise that even if the temptation itself seems pretty harmless, the real issue is not apples or pears, chocolate or stolen kisses, but the state of the human heart. Reflecting on his act of theft, Augustine says that he did not steal the pears to eat them, but just for the sheer, perverse pleasure of doing something that was forbidden.

Dante, an Italian poet of the Middle Ages and author of the *Divine Comedy*, chose more specific examples of temptation. Dante hated bankers, and described usury as one of the principal routes into sin – not merely because of the money itself, but for a more subtle reason. Dante believed that anything that served to mediate between a person and God and made you experience life at one remove was a source of alienation – a separation of oneself from God and from other people, as well as an internal separation within one's own soul. Just as Adam's and Eve's instinctive response to their own sin was the need to take one step back from their intimacy by covering themselves with fig leaves, so Dante understood that sin is anything that ends in losing the ability to approach both God and other people in a direct way, without a degree of protection or separation. This, he believed, was precisely what bankers did as they acted on behalf of their clients, separating people from, rather than reconciling them to, reality. It was therefore the way the banking system removed one's direct contact with one's world that led Dante to believe that usury was a primary sin.

It is usually assumed that Dante calls on the classics as his main source, but interestingly he is far more dependent on the Bible, not only for direct quotes, but for underlying ideas. In the *Commedia* he created a work that was not strictly high art, but not popular media either – it was a middle style that moved between different modes of expression. And this is precisely how the Bible tells its stories, moving backwards and forwards between primitive and sophisticated forms, and covering a wide range of genres, again conforming to Dante's ideal of an unmediated accessibility to God.

≈

Chaucer was writing a generation later, and in England, and here the temptation that led to pride was nearly always taken to be gluttony. The themes of Genesis are woven all through the *Canterbury Tales* (written between 1387 and 1400), but rather than an epic retelling such as Milton's, Chaucer mixes the elements of the biblical narrative rather more obliquely into his tales, so that you have to stay alert to pick up the clues.

The *Canterbury Tales* are a series of stories within a story. A group of pilgrims travel to Canterbury, and to pass the time each of them tells a tale. In between the pilgrims comment on the tales, and on each other's attempts at entertainment and moralisation. Chaucer is thought to have drawn from Boccacio's work, and to have elaborated on various existing tales, and perhaps also some carefully veiled references to controversial events in his own time. The result is a complex mix of stories that reveal human nature, often with a high element of comedy, but also projecting a strong moral theme. Chaucer constantly threads central biblical themes through his stories, which would have been obvious to his readers whose culture was steeped in biblical imagery. For the modern reader, though, it is easy to miss the significance of those references.

The fall of Adam and Eve crops up in a number of Chaucer's tales. The 'Nun's Priest's Tale' is a farmyard tale, told by a chaplain named Sir John, and highlights two things vital to human flourishing: first, avoiding the temptation to fall into pride, and second, the importance of paying attention to your own intuition, which appears in the tale in the form of dreams. On the face of it, the motto of the tale could simply be summed up as 'pride goes before a fall'. But in the course of his tale, Sir John makes a point of placing the story, not simply in the springtime, but thirty-two days after the end of 'that same month wherein the world began, Which is called March, wherein God first made man'.[1] This is a clue to the fact that Chauntecleer's story is linked to Adam's, and the pride he succumbs to is not mere surface vanity, but the sin of pride which led Chauntecleer to think of himself as invincible. If you believe yourself to be great, says the Nun's Priest, you make the same mistake as Chauntecleer, and Adam before him – which is that pride is the essence of all sin and human failure, and ultimately leads to spiritual death. In addition he makes much of the idea that you cannot take advice from a woman, blaming Chauntecleer's downfall on the fact that he listened to his wife instead of his own intuition. This is lifted straight from the pages of Genesis:

> To Adam [God] said, 'Because you listened to your wife and ate from the tree . . . Cursed is the ground because of you . . .'
>
> (Gen. 3:17)

(Eve's role in Genesis has long been used (or misused) to project the idea that women are more gullible, or more culpable, than men. Put simply, it is 'always the woman's fault'. Many twentieth-century writers picked up on the fact that this sentence from Genesis has been used throughout history to keep women in their place.)

Chaucer's readers would also have easily spotted the connection with Genesis in the 'Cook's Tale', which affirms the general opinion of the day that gluttony was one of the chief sins and the temptation that led to Adam's fall and his exile from Eden. It is one of the lesser known of the *Canterbury Tales*, being very brief and possibly unfinished. But even within the *Tales*, the pilgrims give the Cook short shrift. One of the pilgrims, Harry Bailly, assumes the role of judge over the relative merits of the pilgrims' tales, and thus he becomes an authority figure in the story. The link between the 'Cook's Tale' and Genesis is hinted at when the Cook prefaces his own tale by challenging Harry Bailly's authority within the group. He then goes on to tell the tale of Perkyn Revelour, a restless, sexy young man who works as an apprentice to a victualler (a delicatessen or grocer). Perkyn also lives in the victualler's house, and all his needs are taken care of, but the one thing to which he is denied access is the victualler's money box that is kept in the middle of the shop. Perkyn is so taken up with the pursuit of wilder pleasures – dancing, drinking, gambling and womanising – that even though the shop is as full of good things to eat as the garden of Eden, he feels caged in. Eventually he steals money from the forbidden box to go out and enjoy his social life. Just as the forbidden fruit opened up the knowledge of good and evil for Adam,

Perkyn's raid on the hidden treasure opens the way for 'dice, riot or paramour'. The master of the shop, meantime, is a shadowy figure in the background of the tale. Not unlike God in the garden of Eden, we never know his name or see his face; we only know that he would have 'no part of the minstrelcy'. When the victualler discovers Perkyn's crime, his immediate thought – and the one that makes up his mind to banish Perkyn from his shop and his house – is of a proverb about apples. It is better, says the victualler, to remove one rotten apple from the barrel than to let it make all the rest go rotten as well. This puts the spotlight on an important detail – that God banished Adam, not out of pique at being disobeyed, but as damage limitation, so that Adam could not then eat the fruit from the tree of life and live for ever. Perkyn's employer sends him packing to maintain the integrity of his own house and business. To make the parallel with Genesis complete, the 'Cook's Tale' finishes abruptly as Perkyn moves into the house of a 'fallen woman'.[2]

Chaucer later adds a touch of comic effect by adding a story about the 'fall' of the Cook himself. The Cook got so drunk that he fell off his horse and had to be rescued by the other pilgrims. There are three layers going on in the 'Cook's Tale', then. In the background is the fall of Adam and Eve, who defied God, ate forbidden fruit and were expelled from the garden. The 'Cook's Tale' gives us Perkyn Revelour, who disrespects his master but is ultimately undone by gluttony – surrounded by a shop full of good food, and with every need catered for, he still wants what is not really his, and ends up living in poverty with a 'fallen' woman. And the Cook himself begins by challenging Harry Bailly's authority, and ends by having a fall of his own because he too is a glutton and a drunkard.

⇌

East of Eden

Once they had left the garden, we do not hear much more detail about Adam's and Eve's life, beyond the fact that they had descendants. But among the consequences of the fall, God had told Adam:

> By the sweat of your face
>   you shall eat bread,
> till you return to the ground,
>   for out of it you were taken;
> for you are dust,
>   and to dust you shall return.
> (Gen. 3:19 ESV)

This developed into a medieval tradition that while Adam dug the ground, Eve spent her days spinning. A few fourteenth- and fifteenth-century images of this scene have survived, one example being a wall painting (c. fifteenth century) in All Saints Church in Broughton, Huntingdonshire, which shows Adam with a spade, setting about some very stony ground, while Eve sits at her spinning wheel. There is an old rhyme which appears in different versions, one of which is said to be quoted by John Ball in his sermon at the Peasants' Revolt in 1381 to argue for social equality:

> When Adam dolve and Eve span,
> Who was then a gentleman?[3]

It is not unlike a point made in an ancient Jewish commentary – that the reason for having one common ancestral couple was to indicate the equality of all people before God. If everyone is ultimately descended from Adam and Eve, then no one can claim higher descent than anyone else.

The impossibility of return

The idea is lodged deep in Western culture of a lost paradise – a perfect world marred through human misconduct so that relationships are ruptured and the earth goes into rebellion against itself. In all kinds of dramas and stories of this nature there is a tempter or agent of evil who leads the innocent astray, and the beginnings of a route to resolution, forgiveness and restoration. Shakespeare weaves all these themes into *The Tempest*, where a godlike creator figure presides in the background, a woman grows up in complete innocence and is then introduced to a man who gains illicit access to creative powers, and there is a corrupting monster and a fight between good and evil.

The subconscious longing to recapture the lost paradise, and the impossibility of a return to it, is reflected in Coleridge's poem 'Kubla Khan'. Instead of Eden, he takes another mythical, Middle Eastern garden in Xanadu to express the idea that there is a heavenly dimension, a Utopian perfection that the human soul longs for but can never entirely recover. The poem, though, breaks off before the vision is complete, and Coleridge added a note to the poem when it was published in 1816 about its composition, in which he says that he dreamed the whole vision in a nap induced by a painkiller (possibly the laudanum to which he was famously addicted) and on waking, began to write down what he had seen. He was interrupted, however, by a person from Porlock who called him out on business for more than an hour, after which he returned to his poem and found he could not remember the dream. There have been various reactions to this story, some simply dismissing it as typical of Coleridge's excuses for his procrastination. But the truth is just as likely to be that Coleridge created the visitor from Porlock as a fictional character, so that the note and the poem belong together as a whole piece. Read in this way, the poem and its note together encapsulate an idea typical of the Romantic backlash against the empiricism of the Enlightenment, that just because the metaphysical dimension cannot be fully explained, that does not mean it cannot be known at all: it can be glimpsed, even though it can never be fully grasped.[4]

Two centuries later the same theme became common in music. Canadian singer and musician Daniel Lanois reflected on the human capacity for hope and restoration in the midst of unrecoverable loss. In his song 'Maker' he paints a picture of a fractured life, describing himself as first estranged from God and later irresistibly drawn into the healing and essential goodness of 'the Maker'. The joyful undercurrent of this song is about living with your scars, not about a return to unspoilt innocence, which Lanois captures by referring to the gates of Eden, forever closed and guarded by angels, as described in Genesis:[5]

> So the LORD God banished him from the Garden of
> Eden to work the ground from which he had been
> taken. After he drove them out, he placed on the east
> side of the Garden of Eden cherubim and a flaming
> sword flashing back and forth to guard the way to the
> tree of life.
>
> (Gen. 3:23–4)

A similar forward-moving energy, and a quest for something still out of reach, is just one of the biblical themes
that are laced through the music of Irish band U2. Their
song 'I Still Haven't Found What I'm Looking For' clearly
affirms belief in Christian redemption, but suggests that
it is only the beginning and not the end of the story. This
song caused something of a stir among some fans who
hoped that Bono, as a well-known Christian, would deliver
a theology of certainty. But in fact the song is much closer
to the biblical narrative than the rather reductive theolo-
gies of salvation preached by some churches. The Bible
does not really give a picture of salvation as a simplistic
answer to everything, but as a moment in an unfolding
quest.

Cain and Abel

Having left the garden of Eden, sibling rivalry between
Adam's and Eve's sons, Cain and Abel, leads to the first
murder in the Bible:

Now Cain said to his brother Abel, 'Let's go out to the field.' While they were in the field, Cain attacked his brother Abel and killed him.

Then the LORD said to Cain, 'Where is your brother Abel?'

'I don't know,' he replied. 'Am I my brother's keeper?'

The LORD said, 'What have you done? Listen! Your brother's blood cries out to me from the ground. Now you are under a curse and driven from the ground, which opened its mouth to receive your brother's blood from your hand. When you work the ground, it will no longer yield its crops for you. You will be a restless wanderer on the earth.'

Cain said to the LORD, 'My punishment is more than I can bear. Today you are driving me from the land, and I will be hidden from your presence; I will be a restless wanderer on the earth, and whoever finds me will kill me.'

· But the LORD said to him, 'Not so; anyone who kills Cain will suffer vengeance seven times over.' Then the LORD put a mark on Cain, so that no one who found him would kill him. So Cain went out from the LORD's presence and lived in the land of Nod, east of Eden.

(Gen. 4:8–16)

Shakespeare makes specific reference to Cain and Abel in several places. For instance, in *The Merry Wives of Windsor* the expression 'Cain-coloured beard' appears (meaning red-haired), and in *Hamlet* Claudius says,

> It hath the primal eldest curse upon't
> A brother's murder.[6]

But responsibility towards one's family was a matter of particular importance in Elizabethan England, and even without direct reference to Cain and Abel, Shakespeare is often found musing on the extent to which a person was 'his brother's keeper'. The moral questions of jealousy and filial responsibility are the underlying ideas in many of his plays – such as *King Lear*, *Hamlet*, *Othello* and *The Merchant of Venice*, to name a few.

The land of Nod became a common metaphor for sleep after Jonathan Swift punned on the phrase, connecting it to 'nodding off'.[7] Later, in *A Child's Garden of Verses* (1885), Robert Louis Stevenson developed this into the world of dreams:

> Every night I go abroad
> Afar into the land of Nod . . .
> The strangest things are there for me,
> Both things to eat and things to see,
> And many frightening sights abroad
> Till morning in the land of Nod.

The original land of Nod, however, was nothing to do with sleep or dreams. In Hebrew, *nod* means 'wandering', and echoes Cain's miserable words after he murdered his brother that he would forever be a restless wanderer, a fugitive.

The separation between the garden of Eden and the land outside has been used as a metaphor for a lost Utopian ideal. Strictly speaking, though, the biblical narrative never looks back over its shoulder to the lost paradise, but always forwards to a better future. One of the legacies of Christian thought is a linear concept of time, in which you cannot go backwards, and neither does life go round in repeating circles. Instead there is a future yet unimagined, and it is a future of hope, not of despair. John Steinbeck captures this perfectly in his novel *East of Eden*, in which he places his exploration of good and evil, conscience and responsibility, squarely in the world we actually live in, rather than contrasting the real world with a conceptually perfect one. The plot of *East of Eden* has all sorts of parallels with the fall of Adam, beginning with the arrival of Adam Trask, a stranger in a community who is later seduced by a local girl called Cathy, who is a thoroughly bad lot and later abandons Adam and their two sons, Cal and Aaron. The lives of these two brothers mirror those of Cain and Abel, the sons of Adam and Eve (Gen. 4). Cal and Aaron are divided by their work – one works on the land and the other breeds rabbits – and they are caught up in sibling rivalry that eventually leads to tragedy and a crisis of conscience. But the point of these hints and similarities becomes clear at the heart of Steinbeck's novel where Lee, a Chinese cook, expounds his theory as to the interpretation of Genesis 4:7, the words of God to Cain:

> If thou doest well, shalt thou not be accepted? and if thou doest not well, sin lieth at the door. And unto thee shall be his desire, and thou shalt rule over him.
>
> (Gen. 4:7 KJV)

In a nice touch recalling the forbidden fruit, Lee pours Adam and Samuel a glass of a drink that tastes of 'good rotten apples' before he goes on to explain that he has studied intently the meaning of 'thou shalt rule over him' – was it a prediction of fate, a command to be obeyed, or something else?

> 'Don't you see?' he cried. 'The American Standard translation orders men to triumph over sin, and you can call sin ignorance. The King James translation makes a promise in "Thou shalt", meaning that men will surely triumph over sin. But the Hebrew word, the word *timshel* – "Thou mayest" – that gives a choice. It might be the most important word in the world. That says the way is open. That throws it right back on a man. For if "Thou mayest" – it is also true that "Thou mayest not". Don't you see?
>
> '. . . "Thou mayest"! Why, that makes a man great, that gives him stature with the gods, for in his weakness and his filth and his murder of his brother he has still the great choice. He can choose his course and fight it through and win.'[8]

Steinbeck is not particularly interested, then, in comparing sin with an unspoilt perfection. Rather, placing his story 'east of Eden', he explores the idea that we live in a world of free but potent choices, and even when people lack the power to overcome the bad choice, there is the possibility of redemption. For Steinbeck, then, there is no absolving oneself from responsibility by saying it was fate, or 'the devil made me do it'. Rather, good and evil are a matter of 'individual responsibility and the invention of conscience. You can if you will, but it is up to you. This little story (from Genesis) turns out to be one of the most profound in the world.'⁹

⌁

The linear, forwards-moving direction of redemption was also picked up by St Paul, who described Jesus Christ as the 'second Adam'. Just as Adam was seen as the type of fallen humanity, so Paul painted a picture of Jesus Christ as the type of redeemed humanity, but rather than suggesting that this takes us back to the garden, the drift of his argument was that salvation propels humanity forwards to a future that would be even better than the lost Eden. St Paul wrote:

> For since death came through a human being, the resurrection of the dead comes also through a human being. For as in Adam all die, so in Christ all will be made alive. But in this order: Christ, the firstfruits; then, when he comes, those who belong to him.
>
> (1 Cor. 15:21–3)

> So it is written: 'The first Adam became a living being'; the last Adam, a life-giving spirit . . . The first man was of the dust of the earth; the second man is of heaven . . . And just as we have borne the image of the earthly man, so shall we bear the image of the heavenly man.
>
> (1 Cor. 15:45–9)

It is this second Adam who appears in Elgar's *Dream of Gerontius*. John Henry Newman's apocalyptic words describe a soul in a dream-state hanging between life and death, struggling with his own imperfections. He hears five choirs of angels singing from heaven. The fourth choir sing that it was 'by blandishment of Eve, that earth-born Adam fell', but the fifth choir replies:

> O loving wisdom of our God!
> When all was sin and shame
> A second Adam to the fight
> And to the rescue came.
>
> O wisest love! That flesh and blood
> Which did in Adam fail
> Should strive afresh against the foe
> Should strive and should prevail.

Heaven is commonly pictured as a reward for a good life, with images of angels strumming harps on fluffy clouds (although to the modern reader that probably seems a rather dull prospect for eternity!). But what is far more interesting than this caricature is the way in which Christianity has shaped our concept of time – so that heaven represents the idea that life is not just an endless and pointless round of repetitions, but a linear progression with new knowledge to be gained and new adventures to be had. The idea that the future is filled with promise, and expands into hope rather than just endlessly repeating itself, is one of the great legacies of Christian thought.

Noah's ark

Of all the stories in the Bible, Noah's ark is one whose imagery still pervades everyday life. Everything from nursery wallpaper and children's toys to exclusive jewellery carries the image of pairs of animals being loaded onto a comical boat and sailing happily away to sea.

Despite this gentle and comic reading of Noah's ark, the underlying account has elements of horror that rival any natural disaster of recent history. The Asian tsunami that took place on Boxing Day 2004 proved so shocking – not only to the people who were there, but to the whole world – that the anniversary continues to be marked, and the tragic human losses are remembered with appropriate solemnity. Archaeological discoveries have revealed that almost every Mesopotamian culture has a primeval flood myth and, although the details vary, each one tells of a great deluge that wiped out whole populations, leaving only a few survivors. A catastrophe of this magnitude is a terrifying prospect, and it is more than likely that, underneath the layers of religious reasoning, there was a real historical event that people continued to recall decades and even centuries later.

The biblical version begins with the people of the earth being corrupt and living in a reprehensible way that ran counter to the ways of God:

> The LORD saw how great the wickedness of the human race had become on the earth, and that every inclina-tion of the thoughts of the human heart was only evil all the time. The LORD regretted that he had made

human beings on the earth, and his heart was deeply troubled. So the LORD said, 'I will wipe from the face of the earth the human race I have created – and with them the animals, the birds and the creatures that move along the ground – for I regret that I have made them.' But Noah found favour in the eyes of the LORD.
(Gen. 6:5–8)

Noah was the only person who had not lost his moral and spiritual compass, so God told him to build a huge vessel with plenty of accommodation on three levels, a roof on the top and a door in the side, and the whole thing waterproofed with pitch. The dimensions of the ark, measured in cubits, are all recorded in Genesis – 'three hundred cubits long, fifty cubits wide, and thirty cubits high'. Most depictions show some approximation of this structure mounted on top of a conventional boat with a stern and a prow. The Greek myth, though, simply goes with the tea-chest shape, and a recently discovered tablet in cuneiform script describes instructions being given to build something more like a coracle – 'a circular design; Let its length and breadth be the same'.

In the Genesis version, Noah built the ark despite the derision of his neighbours, piled it with great stores of food, and then gathered all the species of animals, seven pairs of some animals, and one pair of all the rest, and herded them onto the ark. Noah and his wife, their three sons and their wives then boarded the ark, still on dry land. And then the floods began:

In the six hundredth year of Noah's life, on the seventeenth day of the second month – on that day all the

> springs of the great deep burst forth, and the flood-
> gates of the heavens were opened. And rain fell on
> the earth forty days and forty nights.
>
> (Gen. 7:11–12)

Noah and his cargo of animals stayed afloat while the flood
continued for 150 days before it began to subside, and then
the mountain tops began to reappear. Then after another
forty days Noah sent out first a raven and then a dove. At
last the dove returned with a twig of an olive tree in its beak,
and Noah knew that the earth was restoring itself. Eventually
Noah opened the door of the ark and found his feet on dry
land. The first thing he did was to give thanks to God, who
in turn promised Noah that never again would the earth be
destroyed. Noah was then instructed to multiply and repopulate the earth, and – as with Adam – there were some rules
set down to protect the new society they would form. With
echoes of the sorry tale of Cain and Abel, there should be
no violence, no murder. And as a sign of God's promise a
rainbow appeared in the sky. Next time it rained, Noah would
see the rainbow and know that it was only rain, not another
flood. 'The Dove and Rainbow' is one of a number of pub
names that are derived from biblical stories, and the dove,
the rainbow and the olive branch are still recognised universally as symbols of peace and used as logos for various causes.

The biblical tale is similar to other ancient flood stories.
There is an ancient Greek myth in which Prometheus puts
his son Deucalion and Deucalion's wife Pyrrha in a large
tea-chest, and they set sail for nine days during which time
everything on earth is flooded except for the summits of
Mount Parnassus and Mount Olympus. They survive on the

37

provisions in the chest until they are able to get out and repopulate the earth.

Even older than Noah's story is a Babylonian poem called the Epic of Gilgamesh, the adventures of King Gilgamesh and his friend Enkidu. After Enkidu's death, Gilgamesh went in search of the secret of immortality, hoping to reclaim his friend from death. On his journey he met Utnapishtim, who told the king he had survived a huge flood after the water god had warned him to build a boat and take his family and friends, animals and valuables. This Babylonian flood legend dates back at least as early as 1750 BC, and it may be the source of the biblical story. The Epic of Gilgamesh was written by a poet in ancient Babylon (in modern-day Iraq) and recorded in cuneiform script on a number of stone tablets. These remained buried for two millennia, until the 1850s, when archaeologists began to unearth them. One version of the Epic was found in the Assyrian royal libraries of Nineveh, and others, written in the Sumerian language, were found as far away as Syria and Turkey. The Epic of Gilgamesh has been translated into English, and revised several times as more ancient sources have come to light.[10]

Over the last couple of hundred years, scholars of various disciplines have mused on the significance of these ancient flood myths. Some rather eccentric expeditions have set out to 'prove' the literal truth of the biblical account by searching for a buried ark on the top of Mount Ararat in Turkey (a project bound to fail as the peak is permanently covered in many metres of ice). But good research never decides its conclusion at the outset, and the more interesting studies have been undertaken by geologists, marine biologists and archaeologists who have taken seriously the possibility that the various primeval flood myths were based on real events lodged in the collective memory. The Genesis account does not merely record weeks of unrelenting rain, but states that 'all the springs of the great deep burst forth' (Gen. 7:11). Instead of assuming this was a fairy story, some scholars have looked here for hints about changes in the geology and water systems of the area. A number of large-scale studies have been undertaken, one instance being Ryan's and Pittman's investigation of a hypothesis that the Black Sea flooded and expanded after a reversal of the current through the Bosporus, and there are indications that the water systems in that area may have changed swiftly and dramatically, causing floods that would have completely washed away any human settlements.

Although it may have its roots in a historical event, like the creation myths the account of Noah's flood is not science or history in the modern sense, but aetiology – a sense-making exercise that tries to say why we are here and what purpose there is for the future. But the meaning of the story has not stood still – it has shifted over time as various aspects have been given more or less emphasis, and for artists it has proved a rich seam to mine. Medieval depictions are often hopeful, such as the beautiful little painting in St Mark's, Venice, of Noah leaning out of the window of the ark with a dove perched on his hand, just about to fly away. In the 'Miller's Tale' Chaucer took all the imagery of Noah's flood and seemingly deliberately misinterpreted it to huge comic effect, with his main character a carpenter abandoned in a bath, and the secrets of God played out in trickster fashion through the inscrutability of a scheming woman. Later depictions of the flood became much darker, with the focus on judgement and catastrophe. Michelangelo's painting in the Sistine Chapel shows masses of people falling into the flood, and the dark horror of the scene is emphasised more in later illustrations – for instance, Gustave Doré's *The Deluge* adds a terrible and hopeless desperation to the faces of those clinging to the rocks amid huge waves.

The scene takes on a somewhat different character in Turner's 1843 painting, *The Evening of the Deluge* (Tate Gallery). Turner conflates the seven days of boarding the ark and the beginning of the storm into one climactic moment, with the animals entering the ark by moonlight amid a gathering storm while Noah and his wife are still asleep in their tent. Rather than focusing on the horror of destruction, Turner conveys an impression of spiritual serenity amid chaos.

Benjamin Britten's children's opera *Noye's Fludde* (1957) does not avoid the tragic elements of the flood either, but here the overall impression is shifted from divine judgement to natural disaster, an effect achieved by adding three congregational hymns to the text of a sixteenth-century mystery play from the Chester Mystery Cycle. One of these was the Victorian hymn 'Eternal Father Strong to Save' by William Whiting, better known as the Naval Hymn, which is often sung at ceremonies for navies and lifeboat services:

> Oh, hear us when we cry to Thee,
> For those in peril on the sea!

In this way Britten handles the fear and mystery of the ocean while viewing the flood victims with more mercy than judgement. And judgement and disaster recede even further in Marc Chagall's *L'Arche do Noé*, where amid chaotic swirls of

Chagall's trademark blue, the impression is of the interior of the ark as a spiritual centre of peace and safety, rather than a contrast between judgement and salvation.

The twentieth century also threw up a number of cheerful interpretations, more in tune with the popular children's version of the story. Hala Wittver's *A Work of Ark* is bright and optimistic, ignoring completely the horror of the devastation in favour of a fantasy ark with a rich garden on deck where two fluffy lambs cuddle up to a mildly annoyed lion, and a wild array of animals get up to all manner of cartoon comedy.

⇌

The Tower of Babel

There is something about building ever-higher structures that captures the human imagination. The Eiffel Tower, the Empire State Building, Canary Wharf, the Burj Khalifa – each of these in its time has been the tallest structure in the world, and no sooner has the last record been broken than the next one is planned.

It seems that the ancient world was no different. Genesis reports that at some point people said, 'Come, let us build ourselves a city, with a tower that reaches to the heavens' (Gen. 11:4). The Tower of Babel, though, ended up not just as a fantastic structure, but as something of a morality tale as well, and in various interpretations it has become a recurring image in art and literature.

As religious fable, the heart of its message is that to set oneself up against God or to attempt to be like God is futile, and that the attempt to make a god of the human race inevitably leads to a collapse of meaning. It has echoes of the garden of Eden – try to be godlike and you end up eating dirt. You could read this as God being pernickety and defensive, but you could equally see it as a story that holds up a mirror to someone's motives: is this person or society trying to find their place in the world, in relationship to others, or trying to be king of the world?

> Now the whole world had one language and a common speech. As people moved eastward, they found a plain in Shinar and settled there.
>
> They said to each other, 'Come, let's make bricks and bake them thoroughly.' They used brick instead of stone, and tar for mortar. Then they said, 'Come, let us build ourselves a city, with a tower that reaches to the heavens, so that we may make a name for ourselves and not be scattered over the face of the whole earth.'
>
> But the LORD came down to see the city and the tower that they were building. The LORD said, 'If as one people speaking the same language they have begun to do this, then nothing they plan to do will be impossible for them. Come, let us go down and confuse their language so they will not understand each other.'
>
> So the LORD scattered them from there over all the earth, and they stopped building the city. That is why it was called Babel – because there the LORD confused the language of the whole world. From there the LORD scattered them over the face of the whole earth.
>
> (Gen. 11:1–9)

Like the creation stories, this seems to have had its roots in Israel's ancient myths. It appears to be set way back in Israel's early tribal history, and is another moral tale to warn against pride. But archaeological discoveries in ancient Babylon suggest that the story may also owe something to the years in captivity – in fact, some have suggested that the story may have originated in Babylon. There was a huge ziggurat in Babylon, called Etemenanki, dedicated to the God Marduk. The similarity of the name Babylon with the Hebrew word *Babel* (which means 'confusion') may have suggested the connection between the story and the location, and the written account in Genesis also details that the tower was built using baked bricks with tar for mortar, which we know was a Babylonian building method, unlike the stone constructions of Judah.

The Babylonian empire was one of the greatest powers of the ancient world, and was at its height under the rule of Nebuchadnezzar II (605–562 BC), extending from the Persian Gulf to Gaza in the west, and from Armenia to the Arabian desert. The walled city at its centre, about 50 miles south of modern-day Baghdad, was perched on the northern banks of the Euphrates river, surrounded by immense city walls six layers deep and containing, as well as the ziggurat, a stunning royal palace and the hanging gardens. So a story about the excessive pursuit of power would certainly have gained new meaning during the Israelites' bruising experience of captivity.

Whatever the origins of the text, the history of art and literature has certainly made much of the tower in its Babylonian setting. For many centuries ancient Babylon was lost beneath the sands of the Persian desert, and artists created images of the tower by using their imagination and their own cultural experience. Illustrated Books of Hours from the fifteenth century often show the tower as a tall, rectangular building with staircases from floor to floor. But the most famous images of the tower are two paintings by Pieter Bruegel the Elder (1563 and 1564–8) in which features reminiscent of the Colosseum in Rome are combined into an immense rising spiral, surrounded by the landscape of sixteenth-century Antwerp. It is not clear whether Bruegel intended his paintings to carry any strong political or religious message. Some have mused on whether the Roman shape of the tower and what appears to be a procession of Catholic priests indicated a criticism of the Catholic Church, and others have speculated that the landscape suggests a sharp message to the people of Antwerp. Either way, Bruegel's spiral tower was recreated by several artists of the Flemish and Dutch schools who followed him, and has also served as the inspiration for some recent reworkings of the idea. In her 2004 work *Babel Revisited* Julee Holcombe, who creates digital photographic compositions based on the old masters, recreated the shapes of Bruegel's tower from a collage of modern-day American skyscrapers. To place these current icons of financial and political success into a traditional image that is doomed to destruction brings sharply into focus the recurring human error of belief in the invincibility of wealth and power.

The Tower of Babel is also central to the recurring idea in Western culture that there was once an original human language, the 'Adamic' language, or the language of Eden, which was the source of all other languages. Dante, however, saw it somewhat differently. He believed that if there were an original language in Eden, it was already extinct before the Tower of Babel was ever begun. For Dante, the significance of the language of Eden was not that it was the first language ever to exist, but that it was the speaker's mother tongue, a mode of communication that was natural, immediate and infused with clarity and mutual understanding. For Dante, the closest one could hope to get to recovering that natural mode of speech was in one's native language, because – as with his reasoning about usury – this removed any artificiality or mediating power between the speaker and God. Dante even believed that the classical languages, usually treated as the languages of perfection and scholarly and artistic clarity, had an element of artificiality about them. When Dante came to compose his *Divine Comedy*, instead of obeying the literary convention of the time and writing in Latin, he chose to follow the new trend for writing in the vernacular languages and composed his work mostly in Italian. The use of the vernacular had begun with the poetry of the Occitan troubadours from Provence (in what is now southern France), and among a number of real characters that Dante included in his journey through the underworld were Virgil, the Roman poet, and Arnaut Danièl, one of the most famous Occitan troubadours, whom Dante met in purgatory. Together they climb up a mountain, symbolically moving closer to God. And at the top of the mountain, just for six lines of the poem, Dante abandons even his native Italian and allows Arnaut to describe his thoughts in his native Occitan. For this, Dante praises Arnaut, saying he is 'the better workman in the mother tongue' – by which he means that to speak in your own dialect is to communicate directly and naturally. He is not suggesting that the vernacular outdoes the classical languages in terms of linguistic skill and sophistication, but that to do something creative with language as it comes naturally to the speaker is creativity at its primary level, and that this is what connects the speaker to God.

The first eleven chapters of the Bible, gathered and edited by the ruling élite of Israel in the fifth century BC, became foundational not only for the future of Israel but also for Christianity, which in turn became central to Western culture. These ancient stories that were seen to encapsulate the human dilemma of alienation from God and ruptured social and personal relationships found their reply and resolution in the story of Jesus Christ, and the idea that he could bring salvation to humanity. These eleven chapters have a disproportionately large influence not only on the art, music and literature that followed in Western culture, but on everything from the concept of time to the development of the legal system, the belief that education mattered, and eventually the pursuit of truth and knowledge that opened up the way for modern science.

3
Father Abraham: The patriarchs of the Old Testament

Up to the end of chapter 11, Genesis follows a repeating pattern: a perfect world that degenerates and then has a new start. But the closing paragraph of chapter 11 marks a gear shift into a long narrative about the founding fathers of ancient Israel.[1] From this point on, God calls one family to find a Promised Land and populate it with people who follow God's ways, so that through them God's blessings would be extended to the whole world.

Abraham's origins were in 'Ur of the Chaldees', from where he travelled with his father's nomadic household to Haran. The location of these places is uncertain, although archaeologists have suggested that this probably describes a journey of a thousand miles or more through modern-day Iran and Iraq.

It is quite a common occurrence in the Bible for people to have their names changed after some life-changing encounter with God – the person's name being changed to mean something that summed up their purpose in life. Abraham started life with the name Abram, and it was not until a solemn covenant was made between Abram and God that his name changed to Abraham, which means 'father of many', and similarly his wife, Sarai, took the name Sarah.

The patriarchal era began when Abram, still living in his father's household, heard God calling him:

> The LORD said to Abram, 'Go from your country, your people and your father's household to the land I will show you.
> 'I will make you into a great nation,
> and I will bless you;
> I will make your name great,
> and you will be a blessing.
> I will bless those who bless you,
> and whoever curses you I will curse;
> and all peoples on earth
> will be blessed through you.'
>
> (Gen. 12:1–3)

This call and promise is pivotal for three of the world's major religions – Judaism, Christianity and Islam – each of which traces its religious identity back to Abraham. Abraham, his son Isaac and his grandson Jacob are the first three generations of this new family of promise, and through the remainder of the Old Testament God is often referred to as 'the God of Abraham, Isaac and Jacob'. The rest of the book of Genesis tells of how God led them into a better life, ordered, prosperous and blessed. It is a story of salvation and blessing based on a covenant or contract between God and his people, and from Abraham it continues to trace its way down the generations.

Was Abraham a real person? Scholars of ancient biblical

history are divided on this point. There is enough correlation between the Bible, other ancient texts and archaeological evidence to place Abraham in the middle to late Bronze Age. Some scholars fiercely defend the oral tradition, pointing out that the content of epics and histories was often so vital to tribal or national identity that, far from being altered in the telling, there was a strict methodology to memorisation and retelling so that it was at least as reliable a form of transmission as the print tradition. So it is likely that there was a real person called Abraham. Others believe he was as much a mythical as a historical figure, and that the stories are apocryphal. The truth may lie somewhere in between. In the same way that we have a mix of history and fable about figures like King Alfred, who was a great English king but who probably did not really burn the cakes, Abraham's story may well be a mixture of history, myth and events attributed to him that really belonged to other people's lives.

You might expect a holy book to be full of highly moral stories about people setting a good example for everyone else. In fact, the patriarchal stories are packed to the gills with dysfunctional families, sibling rivalries and the complicated sexual politics of polygamous households. The descendants that God promised Abram seemed to be a distant dream as he and his wife Sarai (later known as Sarah) grew into old age childless, and eventually Sarai persuaded Abram to take matters into his own hands, and gave him her servant Hagar as a concubine. But no sooner had Hagar produced a son – Ishmael – than Sarai herself miraculously conceived, and their domestic arrangements promptly fell apart. To ensure that her own son, Isaac, was unchallenged as the true heir, Sarai ordered Hagar and

Ishmael out into the wilderness, where they would have been sure to die. The elements of this story have been painted countless times, a number of paintings showing Abraham pointing his finger towards the middle distance and clearly commanding Hagar to leave, some other rather desperate scenes of Hagar and Ishmael thirsty and close to death in the desert, and some more of them being met by angels. Corot combines two of these scenes in *Hagar in the Wilderness* (1835) by placing Hagar and Ishmael in the dark, under the shadow of a rock, while out of their line of sight, in the clear light of day, an angel is winging towards them. Karel Dujardin (1622–78), a Dutch landscape painter, painted *Hagar and Ishmael in the Wilderness* around 1662, the same time that the Book of Common Prayer was published, and his depiction shows not just one angel, but two – an adult angel for Hagar and a little cherub to care for Ishmael. There is also a brilliant life-size sculpture by George Segal (1924–2000), made in 1987, which captures Abraham's hopelessly divided loyalties. The two women are to either side of the scene, Sarah looking on determined and immovable, while Hagar looks away apparently resigned to her fate. Between them Abraham embraces Ishmael with tremendous tenderness before banishing him to his certain death.

The tale of Abraham's domestic strife was set within the wider issues of society, in the shape of Sodom and Gomorrah, the by-word in wicked behaviour and so morally degenerate that, in a kind of throwback to the Noah story, God planned to destroy them – but not before an intriguing dialogue took place. In a scene that Marc Chagall (1889–1985) illustrated in *Abraham Approaching Sodom with Three*

Angels, God appeared to Abraham in the form of three strangers who ate dinner with him and then walked together towards Sodom. Abraham then realised that this was actually God and two angels, in human form.

> When the men got up to leave, they looked down toward Sodom and Abraham walked along with them to see them on their way. Then the LORD said, 'Shall I hide from Abraham what I am about to do? Abraham will surely become a great and powerful nation, and all nations on earth will be blessed through him. For I have chosen him, so that he will direct his children and his household after him to keep the way of the LORD by doing what is right and just, so that the LORD will bring about for Abraham what he has promised him.'
>
> Then the LORD said, 'The outcry against Sodom and Gomorrah is so great and their sin so grievous that I will go down and see if what they have done is as bad as the outcry that has reached me. If not, I will know.'
>
> (Gen. 18:16–21)

Abraham proceeded to argue with God, putting the case for those in the city who were innocent. What if, asked Abraham, there are fifty people in the city who are not corrupt? How could God justify wiping them out with everyone else? And God, in the form of this angelic visitor, agreed that if there were fifty good people in Sodom he would relent. Abraham bartered with God. What if there were forty-five? What if there were only forty? What if there were only thirty, or twenty, or ten? In the event, God relented and some people did escape before the city was destroyed by 'fire and brimstone' (which could be taken simply as God changing his mind, although it is more challenging to read it as an argument against a fatalistic view of the world). Albrecht Dürer's *Lot and His Daughters* (c. 1496/9) shows Abraham's relatives escaping into a calm pastoral scene, while the burning city behind them appears no more frightening than a firework display. But the same scene was given dramatically different treatment by nineteenth-century painter John Martin, whose huge canvasses in the sublime tradition typically showed human figures who were dwarfed by the immensity and power of the natural world. His *Destruction of Sodom and Gomorrah* (1852) shows two figures attempting a seemingly hopeless escape from the horror and heat of an overwhelming volcanic eruption.

The sacrifice of Isaac

There is something unexpected about the idea of God entering into vigorous debate with a mere mortal. Popular caricatures of God tend to show him either as a completely ineffectual old man, or as a wrathful and warlike despot. But the God who actually appears in the Old Testament has a great deal more range than this, and is portrayed almost in a naïve fashion, in direct relationship with these ancient patriarchs. Abraham's God listens to reason and is even willing to change his mind. But only a couple of chapters later, in Genesis 22, we find that the boot is on the other foot, and it is Abraham who has to change his way of thinking in a mysterious tale in which he sets out to sacrifice Isaac, his son and heir, as an act of worship:

> And Abraham rose up early in the morning, and saddled his ass, and took two of his young men with him, and Isaac his son, and clave the wood for the burnt offering, and rose up, and went unto the place of which God had told him.
>
> Then on the third day Abraham lifted up his eyes, and saw the place afar off. And Abraham said unto his young men, Abide ye here with the ass; and I and the lad will go yonder and worship, and come again to you. And Abraham took the wood of the burnt offering, and laid it upon Isaac his son; and he took the fire in his hand, and a knife; and they went both of them together.
>
> And Isaac spake unto Abraham his father, and said, My father: and he said, Here am I, my son. And he said, Behold the fire and the wood: but where is the lamb for a burnt offering? And Abraham said, My son, God will provide himself a lamb for a burnt offering: so they went both of them together. And they came to the place which God had told him of; and Abraham built an altar there, and laid the wood in order, and bound Isaac his son, and laid him on the altar upon the wood. And Abraham stretched forth his hand, and took the knife to slay his son.
>
> (Gen. 22:3–10 KJV)

This scene of child sacrifice is utterly repugnant in any context, but takes on a particular horror when it is overlaid with divine authority. But this scene is set thousands of years ago – probably in the Bronze Age – when it is thought that child sacrifice was common in religious ritual. This might well reflect the normal customs of Abraham's time, but the twist in the tale is the discovery that God was not asking for child sacrifice at all, for just as Abraham was about to slay Isaac, he heard the voice of an angelic messenger telling him not to do it:

> Lay not thine hand upon the lad, neither do thou any thing unto him: for now I know that thou fearest God . . . And Abraham lifted up his eyes, and looked, and behold behind him a ram caught in a thicket by his horns: and Abraham went and took the ram, and offered him up for a burnt offering in the stead of his son.
>
> (Gen. 22:12–13 KJV)

The ram became the sacrifice instead of the boy, and Abraham discovered that the God he worshipped was the God of life, not of death. This drama became a central theme in Christian painting. It is painted onto church walls, such as a seventeenth-century example at Launcells in Cornwall, and appears in paintings by such artists as Rembrandt, Caravaggio and Blake. It was also the subject of a famed competition in Florence at the turn of the fifteenth century, when six sculptors were called upon to submit a bronze panel of the sacrifice of Isaac; the winner would be given the commission to design the bronze doors for San Giovanni in Florence. Vasari, in his *Lives of the Artists*, effusively described Ghiberti's panel as being without defect in design and execution, and also noted that Ghiberti's father had polished the bronze to perfection.[2] Ghiberti himself wrote a similarly effusive account in his *Commentarii*, claiming that not only the judges but even his fellow competitors had conceded that he was the rightful winner. A somewhat different account was given by the biographer of Brunelleschi, one of Ghiberti's rivals, who reported great rivalry and disagreement over the result.

It is a consistent theme throughout the Jewish rabbinic writings that a barbaric death that serves no purpose is against God's will, and that wherever it is possible to do so, God would always choose in favour of life, not death. Genesis 22 is regarded as one of the first stories of the Old Testament to make this idea explicit. But the sacrifice of Isaac throws up psychological questions as well as theological ones, and these were considered by Kierkegaard in *Fear and Trembling*, where he retold the story four times, each with a different ending. First he showed Abraham believing it was God's will to sacrifice Isaac, but telling Isaac it was his own idea, as he would rather Isaac lose faith in his own father than in God. In the second version, despite Isaac being spared at the last moment, Abraham had a crisis of faith over God's original demand that he sacrifice Isaac. The third version showed Abraham refusing to kill Isaac, and praying for God to forgive him for even contemplating such an act. Finally Kierkegaard showed Abraham refusing to kill Isaac, but as a result of his inability to obey God's command, Isaac questioned his own faith.

Although Kierkegaard changed the outcome in psychological terms, he did not change the details of the Genesis account itself. But First World War poet Wilfred Owen gave the story contemporary relevance by reversing the ending to create a tragic irony. He began his poem 'The Parable of the Old Man and the Young' by mimicking the language of the King James Version, 'So Abram rose, and clave the wood, and went . . .' and then recast the scene in the stinking trenches of northern France:

> Then Abram bound the youth with belts and straps,
> And builded parapets and trenches there,
> And stretchèd forth the knife to slay his son.

Owen was among those who believed that the latter phase of the war was prolonged unnecessarily, and that those who had the power to prolong or end the war were simply unwilling to be seen to lose. Borrowing directly from Genesis the words 'Lay not thy hand upon the lad', Owen pictured God pleading with them to lay down their pride instead of seeing many more men slaughtered for little gain. 'Offer the Ram of Pride instead,' pleads Owen's God. But the voice of mercy was never heeded, and by reversing the ending Owen effectively showed the closing months of that war to have slipped into a tragic and bloody slaughter, a battle of pride, not a war of necessity:

> But the old man would not so, but slew his son,
> And half the seed of Europe, one by one.[3]

Stairway to heaven

Isaac, having survived the near disaster of Genesis 22, continued in his father's footsteps as a nomadic shepherd in the Negev, and he in turn fathered two sons – unidentical twins Esau and Jacob. These two were constantly in competition, and Jacob, the younger son, tricked Esau so that he, and not the older brother, inherited his father's blessing and became his heir. As a result of his deceit Jacob decided to put some distance between himself and his brother's anger, and set off in the direction of his uncle Laban's household. Halfway to his destination Jacob lay down in the desert to sleep, using a stone for his pillow, and there he had a dream.

> Jacob left Beersheba and set out for Haran. When he reached a certain place, he stopped for the night because the sun had set. Taking one of the stones there, he put it under his head and lay down to sleep. He had a dream in which he saw a stairway resting on the earth, with its top reaching to heaven, and the angels of God were ascending and descending on it. There above it stood the LORD, and he said, 'I am the LORD, the God of your father Abraham and the God of Isaac. I will give you and your descendants the land on which you are lying. Your descendants will be like the dust of the earth, and you will spread out to the west and to the east, to the north and to the south. All peoples on earth will be blessed through you and your offspring. I am with you and will watch over you wherever you go, and I will bring you back to this land.

I will not leave you until I have done what I have promised you.' When Jacob awoke from his sleep, he thought, 'Surely the LORD is in this place, and I was not aware of it.' He was afraid and said, 'How awesome is this place! This is none other than the house of God; this is the gate of heaven.'

(Gen. 28:10–17)

The connection between climbing up stairs or ladders and gaining access to heaven is found in many ancient cultures. More than fifteen hundred metres in height, Mount Tai, on the Central Plains in China, is one of five sacred mountains. An immensely long stone staircase with 7,200 steps winds up the mountain, and for three thousand years pilgrims have travelled there to make the ascent, which symbolises the journey from earth to heaven. A beautiful gold icon from St Catherine's Monastery shows another stairway to heaven. Based on a spiritual work by St John Climacus, it is called *The Ladder of Divine Ascent*, and shows a ladder stretching diagonally across the painting, with monks climbing up the thirty steps towards the top, where Jesus waits to welcome them. All the way up the ladder they are prayed for by angels, while little demonic stick-figures poke at them to make them lose their balance. A few unfortunate monks topple head first into a pit of darkness, but despite the sober message there is a slightly comic effect in these little characters climbing and falling like pawns in a cosmic game. Snakes and Ladders, the classic board game, became popular in Britain in the late nineteenth century, but has its origins in an ancient and much more complex Indian game called Paramapada Sopanam – The Ladder of Salvation – in which each climb and fall had a specific moral meaning. More recently, Robert Plant of Led Zeppelin had been reading Lewis Spence's *Magic Arts in Celtic Britain* before writing the lyrics to 'Stairway to Heaven'.

All of these depict the climb to heaven as a matter of human effort and determination. But what is interestingly different about Jacob's ladder is that Jacob himself is not challenged to climb up it. Instead he simply has a vision of angels ascending and descending between heaven and earth. For Jacob the stairway is a doorway into heaven, a place of access to the glory of God, but rather than him having to climb up to heaven, it is God who makes the descent. A painting of *Jacob's Dream* by Ribera interprets the scene as a great beam of light shining down on Jacob in an otherwise dark sky. Close up you can see the wispy, shadowy figures of angels in the beam of light.

A second staircase appears in John's Gospel, again as an image of an access route between two different dimensions of reality, when John records a conversation between Jesus and Nathanael, one of his disciples:

> Then Nathanael declared, 'Rabbi, you are the Son of God; you are the king of Israel.'
>
> Jesus said, 'You believe because I told you I saw you under the fig tree. You will see greater things than that.' He then added, 'Very truly I tell you, you will see "heaven open, and the angels of God ascending and descending on" the Son of Man.'
>
> (John 1:49–51)

There is a subtle but important distinction between these various ladders, then. While Christ's disciples were certainly expected to work at their faith, the underlying belief suggests that salvation, or access to God, could not be earned but was a gift from God – an idea that Ribera captures rather well.

Another episode from later in Jacob's life that has inspired artists and sculptors has Jacob wrestling with an angel.

> So Jacob was left alone, and a man wrestled with him till daybreak. When the man saw that he could not overpower him, he touched the socket of Jacob's hip so that his hip was wrenched as he wrestled with the man. Then the man said, 'Let me go, for it is daybreak.' But Jacob replied, 'I will not let you go unless you bless me.' The man asked him, 'What is your name?' 'Jacob,' he answered. Then the man said, 'Your name will no longer be Jacob, but Israel; because you have struggled with God and with human beings and have overcome.' Jacob said, 'Please tell me your name.' But he replied, 'Why do you ask my name?' Then he blessed him there. So Jacob called the place Peniel, saying, 'It is because I saw God face to face, and yet my life was spared.'
>
> (Gen. 32:24–30)

Jacob's words show that he had been with this stranger throughout the night, but he did not realise until the morning that it was God in human form. The nature of the fight has been interpreted in different ways. Delacroix, for instance, shows Jacob setting upon the man in a no-holds-barred brawl. But Rembrandt shows a rather more civilised encounter, which looks like an elegantly choreographed dance. And in Jacob Epstein's huge marble statue, *Jacob and the Angel* (1940–1), the two figures are locked in what looks more like an embrace than a wrestling match. It is Jacob who declares, 'I will not let you go,' but the god-man is holding on to Jacob with more of an air of intimacy than combat. It is reminiscent of the kind of wrestling that sometimes takes place between very close friends or lovers, a struggle that is motivated less by a will to win than a need to be close to each other, the struggle being an internal one rather than a fight for supremacy over the other person. Epstein's Jacob seems loved rather than vanquished, spent and at rest in the arms of God.

Coat of many colours

The very end of Jacob's life sees him blessing his sons, who then become the founders of the twelve tribes of Israel, but the most famous of his heirs was his youngest-but-one son Joseph, whose story still graces the stage today through the Tim Rice and Andrew Lloyd Webber musical *Joseph and the Amazing Technicolor Dreamcoat*.

Joseph was born into the complicated and dysfunctional patriarchal family, rife with arguments over power and inheritance. Jacob had two wives and two concubines, with whom he had thirteen children, but Joseph, although he was Jacob's twelfth son, was the first one born to Jacob's favourite wife, Rachel. (A popular fictionalised account of this polygamous marriage told from the women's point of view is found in *The Red Tent* by Anita Diamant.)

As a young boy Joseph was treated with outrageous favouritism by his father, setting up another family disaster. 'When his brothers saw that their father loved him more than any of them, they hated him and could not speak a kind word to him' (Gen. 37:4).

Like his father before him, Joseph was a dreamer, and within the Bible narrative dreams were taken seriously as a means of hearing divine messages directly from God, or through angelic messengers. Joseph, though, was a very particular kind of dreamer – he dreamed in metaphors and had a God-given gift for interpreting them. Isolated among his brothers by his father's favouritism, Joseph began having dreams about the natural world – one about sheaves of corn and another about the stars in the sky – and in each case the dream represented a vision of a time in the future when Joseph's whole family would bow to his superiority. Lacking somewhat in political diplomacy, Joseph told his brothers about the dreams, with the unsurprising result that they set upon him and nearly killed him. Reuben, the natural heir of the family, brought them back from the brink of murder and persuaded them to leave Joseph in a hole in the ground, his plan being to come back later and take the boy home once he had learned his lesson. But like playground bullying that goes tragically wrong, before Reuben got back the other brothers had sold Joseph as a slave to a passing group of traders who were travelling towards Egypt to sell spices and perfume.

Joseph ended up being sold on as a slave in Egypt, but he was soon promoted in his employer's household: as Tyndale delightfully put it in his 1530 translation, 'the Lorde was with Joseph, and he was a luckie felowe'. Not lucky for long, though, because his employer's wife tried to seduce him, and after he refused her advances she took her revenge by accusing him of sexual assault. Joseph ended up in a dungeon, the ancient equivalent of death row, in the company of the king of Egypt's former cupbearer and baker. These men also had strange dreams of grapes and wine, baskets of bread and thieving magpies. Joseph interpreted their dreams, saying that the cupbearer would return to Pharaoh's service but the baker would be put to death, and sure enough, events turned out just as he predicted. Later, when Pharaoh himself was troubled by recurring nightmares, Joseph was sent for and he interpreted Pharaoh's dreams as meaning that an economic boom would be followed by a deep recession, and that it was essential to lay up supplies in readiness for the coming famine. Joseph then found himself promoted to a senior position in Pharaoh's service, managing the famine relief project.

This whole episode accounts for how the patriarchs, having found their Promised Land, left it again and migrated south to Egypt. Historians tend to think that this narrative was a means of solidifying a national identity with a 'where we came from' story. But, piecing together the historical and archaeological evidence, it seems more likely that the tribes of Israel began from more scattered beginnings – some probably did move north, discontented with life in Egypt, while others were hunter-gatherers living in the hill country around Judea, and others were nomads who eventually settled in the region. Nevertheless, the epic story of Joseph's coat and the dreams, his slavery and imprisonment and the eventual family reunion has proved a rich seam for artists and musicians as well as theologians, and for a whole generation of schoolchildren, Joseph the dreamer will always be remembered as the boy in the Technicolor Dreamcoat.

4
Egypt to the Promised Land

The 1994 movie *The Shawshank Redemption*, based on a novella by Stephen King, begins with Andy Dufresne being imprisoned for a crime he did not commit. Andy serves twenty years inside, but although he is befriended by an older inmate who has become completely institutionalised, Andy secretly works on a plan of escape and never loses his hope of freedom. The key to his escape plan is a hammer hidden inside a Bible, and when this first appears on screen it is no accident that the Bible opens at the book of Exodus. Why? Because Exodus is an epic tale of escape from slavery to freedom, of maintaining hope against despair through seemingly endless years of waiting, and of making a long, arduous journey from imprisonment to redemption. The hero is Moses, one of the towering figures of the Bible, who led the people from Egypt to the Promised Land and along the way received the Ten Commandments.

The epic story of Moses' life begins in the reign of a cruel pharaoh who, in order to limit the numbers of Hebrews in Egypt, sent his men to find and kill every Hebrew infant boy. The mothers and midwives did whatever they could to hide their boys, and Moses' mother put her newborn son into a basket woven from rushes and placed him on the edge of the Nile (this is where the name 'Moses basket' comes from). Watched over from a distance by his sister Miriam, he was found and adopted by Pharaoh's daughter. There are many paintings of this scene, including several in the National Gallery's collection by Orazio Gentileschi (early 1630s), Bartholomeus Breenbergh (1636) and Nicolas Poussin (1651) – each of which illustrates the scene within the conventions of their time. Edward Burne-Jones gives an interesting twist in his drawing *The Finding of Moses* (1879, Tate Collection) by making Miriam central to the drawing, even though she is hidden from the main action of the scene. Burne-Jones's drawing was a cartoon for a predella – a small section from the edge of a stained-glass window that gives a detailed illustration of one aspect of the window's main theme. This window was commissioned for the Church of All Hallows, Allerton, Liverpool, and Miriam is one of four biblical heroines who played a vital, though often overlooked, role in the biblical narrative.

Nothing more was recorded about Moses' early life until, as an adult, he leapt to the defence of a Hebrew slave who was being mistreated and ended up killing the Egyptian guard. He then fled for his life into the desert and married into a family of nomadic shepherds. There he stayed until, years later, he was leading his sheep through the foothills of Mount Horeb when he came upon a strange sight:

> There the angel of the LORD appeared to him in a flame of fire out of a bush; he looked, and the bush was blazing, yet it was not consumed. Then Moses

said, 'I must turn aside and look at this great sight, and see why the bush is not burned up.' When the LORD saw that he had turned aside to see, God called to him out of the bush, 'Moses, Moses!' And he said, 'Here I am.' Then he said, 'Come no closer! Remove the sandals from your feet, for the place on which you are standing is holy ground.'

(Exod. 3:2–5 NRSV)

Mount Horeb is another name for Mount Sinai, and is the mountain that Moses would return to later to receive the Ten Commandments. Centuries later, Constantine's mother, Helena, who had a passion for building chapels on holy sites, had a chapel built at the foot of the mountain on the spot where, according to tradition, Moses had seen the burning bush. This chapel was later incorporated into St Catherine's Monastery, and to this day a shrub traditionally believed to be the bush Moses saw still grows within the monastery enclosure, and anyone entering the chapel is required to remove their shoes before standing on holy ground.[1]

The mysterious image of the burning bush unsurprisingly appealed to William Blake's love of mystical images, and his painting *Moses and the Burning Bush* can be seen in the Victoria and Albert Museum in London. Musing on the origins of the burning bush story, some recent scholars have put forward the theory that hallucinogenic plants may have been used in ancient religious rituals of that region, and that these were the cause of Moses' vision. But ancient writers were untroubled by whether miraculous stories were scientifically possible, and simply took them to be allegorical. Gregory of Nyssa, a writer in the fourth century AD, took the whole life of Moses as an allegory for life, and observed that at the beginning of Moses' journey his encounters with God were characterised by light, but as he aged he tended to meet God in the clouds. Gregory used this to explain why spiritual truth can seem to be a matter of absolute certainty when you are young, but that as life wears on you see truth and wisdom in more and more shades of grey. The closer you get to God, reasoned Gregory, the more you realise that by its very nature, metaphysics is beyond understanding.

According to Exodus, God commissioned Moses to lead the Hebrew slaves out of Egypt, but Pharaoh was reluctant to part with his slave workforce and refused to let them go. In an attempt to persuade him, Moses inflicted ten plagues on Egypt, each one more unpleasant than the last. English painters J.M.W. Turner and John Martin were among those who have painted the various plagues – which included frogs, locusts, flies, the death of cattle and rivers of blood, all of which have been viewed as specific judgements on various Egyptian gods.

The tenth plague was the most horrific of all. Moses warned Pharaoh that if he did not let the people go, God would bring a horrific catastrophe on the Egyptians. But Pharaoh was unmoved. Moses then went to prepare the Hebrews for their escape. They made bread without yeast for the journey, and then put a mark on each of their door lintels.

> And the LORD said unto Moses, Yet will I bring one plague more upon Pharaoh, and upon Egypt; afterwards he will let you go hence: when he shall let you go, he shall surely thrust you out hence altogether . . .

Moses was very great in the land of Egypt, in the sight
of Pharaoh's servants, and in the sight of the people.
And Moses said, Thus saith the LORD, About midnight
will I go out into the midst of Egypt: And all the firstborn in the land of Egypt shall die, from the firstborn
of Pharaoh that sitteth upon his throne, even unto the
firstborn of the maidservant that is behind the mill;
and all the firstborn of beasts. And there shall be a
great cry throughout all the land of Egypt, such as
there was none like it, nor shall be like it any more.

(Exod. 11:1, 3–6 KJV)

Later that night, in an echo of the slaughter that Moses
himself had survived as a baby, the firstborn son of every
Egyptian household died. But the plague of death passed
over the Hebrew homes with the marked doors – hence the
name Passover for the Jewish feast – and while Egypt
mourned her sons, the Hebrews walked out of Egypt, across
the Red Sea and through the desert towards the Promised
Land, the land of milk and honey. The Exodus remains
central to Jewish identity to this day, and is also claimed by
Christians as an allegory of the salvation that God would
later bring through Jesus.

The terrible stories of the plagues are among those that
have led to the caricature of an Old Testament God who is
wrathful and merciless – almost as if God went through a
character change between the Old Testament and the New.
The Bible is actually more complex than that, with countless
acts of kindness alongside the horror stories. But it is also
worth considering that the plagues might seem justified
depending on your point of view. And the stories of God's

wrath on the Egyptians made perfect sense to another group of people in modern history, who took them as an allegory of their own situation.

The so-called 'Negro spirituals' emerged out of the long and shameful history of slavery in the eighteenth and nineteenth centuries, when those who suffered unimaginable and inhumane treatment adopted these ancient stories as their songs of hope. Slaves were forbidden to read or write or to gather in groups, but it is a testament to the human spirit that despite their desperate circumstances they refused to stop singing. 'Go Down Moses' is thought to have been a song of the contrabands of the 1860s, made famous through recordings by Paul Robeson and Louis Armstrong:

> When Israel was in Egypt's land:
> Let my people go.
> Oppress'd so hard they could not stand:
> Let my people go.
> Go down, Moses,
> Way down in Egypt land,
> Tell old Pharaoh,
> Let my people go.

Go Down Moses was also the title of a book by William Faulkner – seven short stories that together make up a fragmented novel tracing the fortunes of a plantation family in Mississippi.[2] Faulkner skilfully connects the oppression of the Jews in Egypt with that of the slaves in the American South, and although the book does not shy away from the ugly realities of prejudice and exploitation, it also casts some rays of hope for the possibility of change.

In the twentieth century, English composer Michael Tippett incorporated a number of spirituals into his oratorio *A Child of Our Time*, the title of which was taken from an anti-Nazi novel by German writer Odon von Horvath. Tippett was a pacifist and a humanist, and his oratorio was written in response to one tragic story from the Second World War. Herschel Grynszpan was a young Polish Jew who was living in Paris with his uncle and aunt. One day in November 1938 he set out to assassinate the German ambassador as an act of revenge for the expulsion of thousands of Polish Jews, including his own family. But for reasons that are not clear, after waiting outside the embassy for some time, Grynszpan instead shot a minor official who died soon afterwards. It was this murder that triggered the event that became known as Kristallnacht, or the 'Night of Broken Glass'. On the night of 9 November 1938, throughout Germany, Austria and parts of Czechoslovakia, the Nazis organised a terrifying night of retribution. Thousands of Jewish shops were destroyed, their windows smashed in, and 400 synagogues were burned down. Ninety-one Jews died and thousands were sent to concentration camps. Tippett, although not a religious man himself, found that the agonised cry for freedom in the spirituals gave expression to yet another event in history where a whole race was severely oppressed and threatened with extinction. Using Handel's *Messiah* and Bach's Passions as his model, he gave the spirituals a similar function to Bach's chorales, punctuating the narrative with cries of anger and outrage at injustice. Although Tippett's spirituals are sometimes sung separately, as 'Five Spirituals', it is only in the context of the oratorio that they express the meaning with which Tippett invested them.

It is possible to walk from Egypt to Israel across the Sinai desert in a matter of days, but Exodus describes the Hebrews taking a long and circuitous journey through the desert for forty years, learning lessons about life and faith, before they finally reached the Promised Land. Along the way Moses became the lawgiver by climbing up Mount Sinai once again to receive the Ten Commandments, engraved by God on two tablets of stone. The story is repeated several times (in Exod. 20:2–17; 34:12–26; Deut. 5:6–21) from different points of view. Having received the Ten Commandments, Moses came back down the mountain only to discover that the people had melted down their jewellery to make a golden calf, an object of worship in ancient Egypt. In a furious rage, Moses smashed the tablets of stone and rebuked the people, before setting off up the mountain a second time to apologise to God and plead for a second chance to receive the commandments. Paintings of Moses often show him about to smash the first stone tablets in anger. Unsurprisingly, neither William Blake nor John Martin could resist the apocalyptic fury of Moses, and their paintings of him belong to the Tate Collection (William Blake, *Moses Indignant at the Golden Calf*, 1799/1800; John Martin, *Moses Breaketh the Tables*, 1833, Tate Collection). Rembrandt's *Moses with the Ten Commandments* (c. 1659) shows Moses with the tablets lifted up, although it is not clear whether he is teaching them or about to smash them.

The laws recorded in the Old Testament are long and complex, filling three further books – Numbers, Leviticus and Deuteronomy. But the Ten Commandments – four instructions about worshipping God, and six rules outlining a basic social contract – stand as the summary and the iconic image of the law. Many churches have the Ten Commandments painted onto the walls, underlining the central importance of them as a moral code in English history. Many of the principles of British law are also derived from the biblical laws – for instance, the equality of all people before the law.

There is a surprise element at the end of Moses' story. At long last, having taught the people the whole of the law and covenant, he brought them safely to the borders of the Promised Land. But at the last minute he handed over the reins to his successor, and then died, leaving the people to start their new life under Joshua's leadership.

Although the events of Moses' life gave artists, musicians and movie-makers plenty of epic stuff to play with, some artists simply wanted to portray the idea of Moses. One of Turner's loveliest lightscapes, *Light and Colour (Goethe's Theory) – The Morning After the Deluge – Moses Writing the Book of Genesis* (1843, Tate Gallery, London) ignores any concerns about the order of the biblical narratives, still less historical reality, and conflates the stories of the five books of the Torah to show Moses writing the book of Genesis in a whorl of light, supposedly the day after the deluge. But my own favourite portrait of Moses is by R.B. Kitaj and appeared in the Royal Academy's 2008 Summer Exhibition. *Moses Contra Freud* (2005) shows a wizened, elderly face lined with the patience, kindness and wisdom of someone who knows that the letter of the law is not enough: it can only work in the context of generous human relationship.

＝

After the death of Moses, Joshua led the people into the Promised Land – Canaan, the land flowing with milk and honey. One of the first stories of the conquest is the famous tale of the Battle of Jericho.

Now Jericho was tightly shut up because of the Israelites. No-one went out and no-one came in.

Then the LORD said to Joshua, 'See, I have delivered Jericho into your hands, along with its king and its fighting men. March around the city once with all the armed men. Do this for six days. Make seven priests carry trumpets of rams' horns in front of the ark. On the seventh day, march around the city seven times, with the priests blowing the trumpets. When you hear them sound a long blast on the trumpets, make all the people give a loud shout; then the wall of the city will collapse and the people will go up, every man straight in.'

. . . They did this for six days.

On the seventh day, they got up at daybreak and marched around the city seven times in the same manner, except that on that day they circled the city seven times. The seventh time around, when the priests sounded the trumpet blast, Joshua commanded the people, 'Shout! For the LORD has given you the city! The city and all that is in it are to be devoted to the LORD . . .

When the trumpets sounded, the people shouted, and at the sound of the trumpet, when the people gave a loud shout, the wall collapsed; so every man charged straight in, and they took the city.

(Josh. 6:1–20 NIV)

Jericho is a real place. Today it is a small modern town in the Jordan valley, fifteen miles north-east of Jerusalem, but nearby is a hill which, as you get closer, you realise is not a natural hill but a tell – the many layers of the remains of ancient Jericho. Archaeological evidence shows that the city was abandoned, expanded and rebuilt several times over, but as its location on the Jordan river made it a stop on a major trade route, as well as a source of water in a hot dry climate, it is not surprising that Jericho was fought over repeatedly.

The excavation of old Jericho led to lengthy debates over the dates of the ancient city. Charles Warren did a site survey in 1868, in order to map the sites to which the biblical place names referred. German archaeologists carried out a more extensive dig of the site between 1907 and 1911, and concluded that Jericho had already been abandoned by the time of the biblical conquest. Another dig in the 1930s revealed a series of collapsed walls and raised the possibility that the walls of the city really had fallen down. In the 1950s, with new archaeological methods at her disposal, Kathleen Kenyon carried out new excavations and created a timeline of the entire history of the settlement, going right back to its origins in the Stone Age. Kenyon's findings are still generally accepted, and Jericho is claimed to be the world's oldest known continuously occupied settlement, dating back at least as far as 9000 BC and possibly earlier. There was evidence of an established agricultural economy, and it is thought that it may also have been the earliest walled city as there was a large wall and a tower dating from about 7000 BC. Kenyon estimated that the destruction of Jericho took place around 1425 BC.

The excavation of Jericho illustrates just how difficult it is to establish the details of ancient history. But the story of this much fought-over city has resonated down the centuries, and in the same way that even fictitious stories can tell the truth, something at the heart of these old tales rings true despite uncertainties of historical detail.

Like 'Go Down Moses', Joshua also became the inspiration for a spiritual.

> Joshua fit de battle of Jericho, Jericho, Jericho,
> Joshua fit de battle of Jericho, and the walls came a
>   tumbalin' down.
> You may talk about your men of Gideon,
> you may talk about your men of Saul,
> but there's none like good old Josh-a-ua,
> at the battle of Jericho.

Judges

When the people first entered the Promised Land, they were not yet a unified nation with a king, but an amalgamation of tribes which loosely divided into two groups – the larger being Israel in the north, and a smaller group of southern tribes which became known as Judah. Kings, according to the biblical narrative, were what other nations had, while the Israelites lived as a theocracy where only God was their 'king'. In reality, they were probably small tribes with local leaders, and the drive for a king only came later as the tribes increasingly functioned together as a larger unit. But in the meantime the local leaders were called judges, and they gave their name to the next book in the Bible.

Gideon

Most people will at some time or other have come across a Gideon Bible in a hotel or conference centre. The organisation that puts them there is named after Gideon, who was one of the judges of the Old Testament. Gideon was one of the most reluctant rulers ever. Fearful and completely lacking in confidence, he saw himself as the weakest man from the weakest tribe. Faced with an attack from the Midianites, an aggressive neighbouring tribe, the people looked to Gideon to lead them out of trouble. Gideon asked God for a series of miraculous signs as proof that he would win. He put a sheep's fleece outside overnight, and said that in the morning, if the ground was dry but the fleece was wet, then he would know that God was with him and he should go into battle. In the morning the fleece was wet and the ground was dry. But Gideon was still racked with doubt, and asked God to do the same in reverse – that the ground would be wet with dew, but the fleece dry. Again, the miracle took place, and Gideon went into battle and won the day.

The old saying 'putting out a fleece' – meaning to look for a sign to help you make a decision – comes directly from this story. But Gideon's fleece also gained a more tangential set of meanings. In medieval times dew was taken to be a metaphor for fertility, and the liturgy of the Church connected the dew falling on Gideon's fleece (Judges 6:36–40) with a prophecy from Isaiah: 'Drop down, ye heavens, from above, and let the skies pour down righteousness: let the earth open, and bring forth a saviour' (Isa. 45:8). These two biblical quotes were used during Advent and the feast of the Annunciation as a meditation on the conception and birth of Christ. A Middle English antiphon for Prime reads, 'When he was born wonderfully of a maid, then was fulfilled Holy Writ: dew came down like rain into a fleece for to make safe mankind.'

Samson

If Gideon was the weakest of the judges, then the last and most famous of the judges, Samson the Nazirite (Judg. 13 – 16), was renowned for being the strongest man in the world. He killed a lion with his bare hands, and single-handedly won a fight with thirty men. The secret of his strength, according to the Bible, lay in a vow made before God never to cut his hair (although reading between the lines he also had a pretty ferocious temper). But he made an ill-advised marriage with Delilah, who was from the enemy tribe of Philistines. Delilah sweet-talked Samson into telling her his secret, which she then used treacherously against him. Her brothers came in while Samson slept, cut his hair and gouged out his eyes, so that they could take the political advantage over the Israelites. What they did not foresee, though, was that when Samson's hair grew back his strength returned, and even in his reduced and humiliated state he was able to bring about a revenge killing. It is not a pretty story, but it has all the visual drama of a grand Greek myth or an Icelandic saga, and is the inspiration for John Milton's 1671 drama

Samson Agonistes, Handel's oratorio *Samson* (1743) and Saint-Saëns' opera *Samson et Dalila* (1835–1921). Delilah's betrayal is shown in paintings by Rubens (*Samson and Delilah*, c. 1609–10, National Gallery, London), Rembrandt (*Samson Betrayed by Delilah*, c. 1629/30, oil on panel, Gemäldegalerie, Berlin), and Pompeo Batoni (*Samson and Delilah*, 1766, The Metropolitan Museum of Art). The allusion to the biblical Delilah is unavoidable in Tom Jones's 1960s pop song of the same name, a modern-day tale of love, betrayal and a crime of passion. Samson's strength was alluded to in Procul Harum's song 'Strong as Samson', and his name is still regularly adopted as a trade name for everything from extra-strong rope to heavy-duty security doors.

=

Zadok the priest and the kings of Israel

A grainy black-and-white newsreel of a June day in 1953 showed millions lining the streets of London to catch a glimpse of the young Queen Elizabeth as she passed by in her carriage. A congregation of eight thousand gathered in Westminster Abbey and stood as the young queen entered the abbey and processed up the aisle, the train of her crimson coronation robe carried behind her by six ladies in waiting. The cameras were there to record the moment: it was only the second coronation ever to be televised, and for the first time ever, more than just a select few were enabled to see the most solemn parts of the coronation ritual that took place beyond the screen. After she had sworn the solemn oaths, the queen's crimson robe was removed and she was dressed in the golden anointing robe and seated in King

Edward's Chair, the chair on which kings and queens of England have been crowned for centuries. There she received the orb and sceptre, the rod of justice, the royal ring and the crown, and then cries of 'God save the Queen' were heard throughout the abbey.

Some of the music played that day was written specially for the ceremony, but one piece of music was the same as at every coronation since 1727. The steady throb of string arpeggios gradually built the tension through the long orchestral introduction, moving through scrunches of sound as the chords resolved and unresolved repeatedly, until at last, in a great *coup de théâtre*, the choir burst in with a huge wall of sound: 'Zadok the priest, and Nathan the prophet, anointed Solomon king.'

Zadok the Priest was the first of four anthems written for the coronation of George II on 11 October 1727. Music for coronations was usually written by the organist and composer of the Chapel Royal, but it so happened that in 1727 the post was in an interregnum, and thus it was that George Frederick Handel, who had already written the *Water Music* for the royal family, was commissioned to compose music for the occasion. Such was the grandeur of the event that Handel found himself with a far larger number of singers and musicians at his disposal than he was accustomed to, with a choir of more than forty singers and an orchestra that reportedly numbered 160.

An anthem entitled *Zadok the Priest* had previously been written by Henry Lawes for the coronation of Charles II in 1661, and was played again when King James was crowned. But Lawes' composition was eclipsed by Handel's, which quickly became one of the most popular pieces in the repertoire of English ceremonial music. It has been played at every coronation since 1727, and at countless celebratory occasions up and down the land – weddings, graduations, concerts and proms. It is heard on popular music stations nearly every day of the year, and has even been 'borrowed' and remixed as the UEFA Champions League anthem, played during pre-game match ceremonies and as the intro-duction to television coverage of the event.

Behind the anthem, though, lies the coronation of Solomon, the third king of Israel, and one of the most famous and revered kings of the ancient world. It is a story of polit-ical intrigue and a dash for the throne that left no time for well-planned ceremonials like those in Westminster Abbey. This is how it came about.

The first king of Israel was Saul, an ordinary and rather self-effacing man who seems to have been made king mostly because he was tall and handsome. But his son Jonathan did not succeed him. In the biblical narrative kings became kings not merely through inheritance, nor as the result of political victory, but through divine appointment (see 1 Sam. 16:1), conferred by anointing with oil in a religious ceremony – a point we shall return to in a moment. Instead of Jonathan, it was David who became the second king of Israel – David who had been a mere slip of a shepherd boy when he conquered Goliath the giant with nothing more than a few stones in a sling. David's youthful perfection was immortal-ised in Michelangelo's sculpture *David* in the Galleria dell'Accademia, Florence, sculpted between 1501 and 1504.

Fast-forward to the end of David's life. David had a long-standing promise to his favourite wife Bathsheba that their son, Solomon, would succeed him as king of Israel. But in family terms, Solomon was not the first in line for the throne. David's favourite son, Absalom, died in a revolt when he tried to overthrow his father and take the throne for himself (a story which itself has inspired a good deal of art and literature, including the motet *Absalon, fili mi*, written about 1497 and attributed to Josquin des Pres, Leonard Cohen's *Prayer for Sunset*, and novels about complex father-son relationships such as *Absalom! Absalom!* by William Faulkner and *Cry, the Beloved Country* by Alan Paton). With Absalom out of the picture, the way to the throne was open to David's next son, Adonijah. As David's death approached, Adonijah saw his moment of opportunity and, rather than wait for his father to take the initiative in naming him as the next king, he set about effecting his own coronation.

Two of David's closest advisors were Zadok the priest and Nathan the prophet. Nathan heard about Adonijah's plan, but, wise man that he was, rather than go directly to the frail king he went instead to the power behind the throne, Bathsheba, told her about the conspiracy and then sent her in to appeal to David, who promptly ordered his men into action to crown Solomon without delay.

> So Zadok the priest, Nathan the prophet, Benaiah son of Jehoiada, the Kerethites and the Pelethites went down and had Solomon mount King David's mule, and they escorted him to Gihon. Zadok the priest took the horn of oil from the sacred tent and anointed Solomon. Then they sounded the trumpet and all the people shouted, 'Long live King Solomon!' And all the people went up after him, playing pipes and rejoicing greatly, so that the ground shook with the sound.

Adonijah and all the guests who were with him heard it as they were finishing their feast. On hearing the sound of the trumpet, Joab asked, 'What's the meaning of all the noise in the city?'

Even as he was speaking, Jonathan son of Abiathar the priest arrived. Adonijah said, 'Come in. A worthy man like you must be bringing good news.'

'Not at all!' Jonathan answered. 'Our lord King David has made Solomon king. The king has sent with him Zadok the priest, Nathan the prophet, Benaiah son of Jehoiada, the Kerethites and the Pelethites, and they have put him on the king's mule, and Zadok the priest and Nathan the prophet have anointed him king at Gihon. From there they have gone up cheering, and the city resounds with it. That's the noise you hear.'

(1 Kgs 1:38–45)

Unlike modern-day coronations, when Solomon was anointed king of Israel there was no time to adjust the robes, commission special music, gather the crown jewels, plan a reception and send out invitations. It was a last-minute dash for the throne with just the bare essentials – the royal mule for transport, the oil for anointing, and a prophet and a priest to carry out the ceremony.

But despite the differences between this ancient story and the coronations where Handel's anthem is sung, there is one similarity, and perhaps it is a surprising one in an increasingly secularised culture. For in 1953, the ritual of anointing with oil and the ceremonial handing over of a sceptre and an orb carried the implication that the authority of the monarch is still conferred by God, and not merely an accident of history.

⇌

Another of Handel's works, the *Arrival of the Queen of Sheba*, has been the accompaniment for many a modern bride as she has processed in or out of her wedding. Composed in 1748 as an instrumental interlude from Handel's oratorio *Solomon*, it has since been rearranged for various instrumental combinations. Solomon was renowned in the ancient world for his long and peaceful reign, the great wealth and success of his kingdom, and more than anything for his wisdom. Under Solomon's rule the northern and southern tribes of Israel were united into one kingdom for the first time, and foreign powers bowed to his supremacy and sought to visit his great palace and the temple he built. Centuries later, in the sixteenth century, the final stages of building and embellishment of King's College Chapel in Cambridge were completed during the reign of Henry VIII. There among the stained-glass windows, Solomon appears seated on his throne, attended by a respectful Queen of Sheba. But it is difficult to avoid the fact that Solomon bears a striking resemblance to Henry himself, with his large square face, his trademark Tudor sleeves and the soft square cap that was the ancestor of the academic 'mortar board'. Henry had inherited a stable and wealthy realm from his father, Henry VII, who had successfully united the houses of York and Lancaster. And so Henry VIII is depicted as a latter-day Solomon – a great monarch with his kingdom united, renowned among foreign powers for his wealth, success and wisdom.

Ancient Israel never again enjoyed the degree of cohesion and peace that they found under Solomon's rule. The remainder of the history of Israel alternated between periods of blessing and times of suffering, which were put down to whether or not the king led the people to worship and obey God. Throughout this part of the Bible the chief advisors to the kings were the prophets, whose role was to be the spiritual guide of the people of Israel, to pray for the nation and to speak the truth. The prophets were advisors without a portfolio – answerable first to their convictions, and uniquely able to be the opposite of a 'yes-man'. For this reason they were often unpopular with the bad kings, the ones who turned to worship other local gods, or who were more interested in lining their own pockets than in leading their people.

There is more to tell of the history of Israel, her prophets, priests and kings, and how their fortunes rose and fell in the years before and during the exile in Babylon. If you continue to read the Bible straight through, it gets rather confusing at this point, because what has seemed approximately chronological thus far is suddenly completely disrupted. First the books of Chronicles retell much of the story of the kings. Then the books of Ezra and Nehemiah relate what happened after the exile. In between there are a few stand-alone biographies, which are more like morality tales than histories. And later there is another rewind to the eighth century BC and the pre-exile story is retold, not by historians, but by the prophets themselves. But before that there are five books that are not history at all, but are collectively known as the books of wisdom. That will be the subject of the next chapter.

5
Hallelujah

Right in the middle of the Old Testament is the book of Psalms, which is a collection of 150 songs. Although their tunes have not survived, among the words appear a few markers that seem to be musical instructions – such as where the chorus is repeated, or where there is a pause or an instrumental break. The Psalms are unique among the books of the Bible in that they are addressed directly to God as songs of worship, hymns of victory, sorrowful laments and grand arguments with God. Quite a bit of the phraseology of the Psalms has found its way into everyday English language, and some of the psalms have become known as classic poems, renowned musical works and even the occasional pop song.

The word *Hallelujah* has been in use for at least three thousand years. Often the first or the last word of a psalm, it appears more often than any other word in the book of Psalms. Its consonants are soft rather than guttural, and the vowels are long and open, making it a supremely sing-able word. Its literal meaning is 'praise the Lord', but it can be given a wide range of emotional meaning, not least because the sounds ooh, aah and ay are used the world over as spontaneous expressions of feeling, and in exclamations like 'hurrah', 'phew' and 'yay'. By choosing where to place the emphasis, a composer can equally make 'Hallelujah' an expression of joy, triumph, relief or sorrow. Handel's 'Hallelujah Chorus' is undeniably joyful and exhilarating, and in the context of his oratorio it also expresses relief after distress. But Leonard Cohen put the 'aah' and 'ooh' of 'Hallelujah' into a melody that describes the repeated rise and fall of a minor third within a perfect fourth, creating a mournful tone. Cohen's original rendition of 'Hallelujah' had an element of defiance in the face of sadness, but Jeff Buckley's cover[1] was arguably even more poignant than the original, his pure, haunting voice drawing out the lamenting quality of the song.

The language and phraseology of the Psalms is reproduced frequently in literature. St Augustine, for instance, quoted extensively from Scripture in his work, but in his *Confessions*, which like the Psalms is addressed directly to God rather than to the reader, he draws the largest number of his quotes from the Psalms. Shakespeare also draws on biblical language and ideas, and although he makes use of Genesis and the Gospels to some extent, it is the Psalms that run like a thread through his work. By the time Shakespeare was writing, the Psalms had already been translated by Miles Coverdale, a writer with a supreme gift for poetic language and who, in 1535, became the first person to publish a complete English translation of the Bible. Coverdale's translations of the Psalms were published as a separate Psalter, and his phraseology survived into several later English translations of the Bible, including The Great Bible (1539) and The Bishops Bible (1568).

By the rivers of Babylon

Psalm 137 is probably best known in present-day culture through the song 'By the Rivers of Babylon' by 1970s disco band Boney M. It was the top-selling single in the UK in 1978, and has been remixed, re-released and covered by numerous artists ever since. But it was also one of the best-known psalms of the seventeenth century, and its themes and language appear in the work of various writers of the period, including Milton, Spencer, Johnson and Shakespeare.

In the 1568 Bishops Bible, with which Shakespeare was familiar, this is how Psalm 137:5–6 appears:

> If I forget thee O Hierusalem: let my right hande forget [her cunning.] Let my tongue cleaue to the roofe of my mouth, if I do not remember thee: yea if I preferre not thee O Hierusalem aboue my most myrth.

> *If I forget you, Jerusalem,*
> *may my right hand forget its skill.*
> *May my tongue cling to the roof of my mouth*
> *if I do not remember you,*
> *if I do not consider Jerusalem*
> *my highest joy.*

> (TNIV)

The idea that alienation makes you unable to sing or to speak was a powerful one in the sixteenth and seventeenth centuries – bearing in mind, of course, that to be exiled to a foreign land at that time was a far more isolating experience than our modern understanding allows. In *Richard II*, when Thomas Mowbray, Duke of Norfolk, is banished for life, he realises that he will never again live in a place where his native English is spoken. His speech from Act 1, Scene 3 expresses the extreme alienation of this punishment:

> The language I have learnt these forty years,
> My native English, now I must forgo,
> And now my tongue's use is to me no more
> Than an unstringed viol or a harp,
> Or like a cunning instrument cas'd up –
> Or being open, put into his hands
> That knows no touch to tune the harmony.
> Within my mouth you have engaol'd my tongue,
> Doubly portcullis'd with my teeth and lips,
> And dull unfeeling barren ignorance
> Is made my gaoler to attend on me.
> I am too old to fawn upon a nurse,
> Too far in years to be a pupil now:
> What is thy sentence then but speechless death,
> Which robs my tongue from breathing native
>   breath?

The direct use of the biblical language is clear – Shakespeare's description of the 'cunning instrument' and the hands that cannot play is a direct reference to 'let my right hande forget her cunning', and his tongue being 'engaol'd' behind 'teeth and lips' is reminiscent of 'Let my tongue cleaue to the roofe of my mouth', a phrase that appears again later in the play (Act 5, Scene 3) when Aumerle entreats Bolingbroke, who spent six years in exile and has now returned with his own claim on the throne, to forgive him for his treason:

> For ever may my knees grow to the earth,
> My tongue cleave to my roof within my mouth,
> Unless a pardon ere I rise or speak.

The Lord is my shepherd

Psalm 23 is the best known of the psalms and is regularly sung in both Jewish and Christian religious ceremonies. It is seen both as an encouragement in life and as a comfort in death, so it is sung both at weddings and funerals, and is recited at hospital bedsides, and the comforting power of the words seems to extend way beyond their religious context. Certainly its themes are reassuring, but its power is attributable not only to its religious meaning but also to the beauty of the English translation.

In a number of surviving Middle English Psalters (from about 1250 to 1400) the fourth verse of the psalm is translated quite correctly from the Latin to mean 'in the midst of the shadow of death'.

> ife I ga in mid schadw ofe dede
> > (The Surtees Psalter, probably from Yorkshire,
> > c. 1250–1300)

> if i had gane in myddis of the shadow of ded
>> (Richard Rolle, probably c. 1335)

> For if þat ich haue gon amiddes of þe shadowe of
> deþ
>> (West Midlands Psalter, c. 1350)

> For whi and if I shal go in the middel of the
> shadewe of deth
>> (Wycliffe's early version, c. 1380)

Miles Coverdale, though, when he came to translate the psalm, showed his surpassing poetic talent by rewording this as 'Yea, though I walk through the valley of the shadow of death' – a phrase that no translator since has been able to improve upon.

Coverdale produced his English version of the Psalms some seventy years before the publication of the King James Bible. Prior to this, apart from a few excerpts, the Bible had been available only in Latin or Greek, so for more than a thousand years most people had not been able to understand the Bible unless a priest explained it to them. Coverdale was among a group of Protestant rebels who were convinced that the Bible should be available in the vernacular languages of Europe, but not everyone was of the same opinion. Many of the fifteenth- and sixteenth-century translators were persecuted, some went into exile, and some were even executed for heresy. One of Coverdale's mentors was William Tyndale, who was condemned to death, half-strangled and then burned at the stake. So when Coverdale coined the phrase 'the valley of the shadow of death' he had more in mind than poetic beauty or metaphysical musings – it was a daily reality for this generation of Reformers and Bible translators.

One of the subsequent English versions of the Bible was known as the Geneva Bible because its translators had gone into exile in Geneva for their own safety. In Coverdale's case, it seems that much of his translation work was carried out in an attic in Antwerp. Not schooled in Greek and Hebrew, he worked from Luther's German translation and the Latin Vulgate. But despite the fact that his was an indirect translation, the beauty of his poetry continued to be used in Anglican prayer books until the late twentieth century.[2]

The twenty-third psalm has been set to music many times. A metrical version (an arrangement of the words into a rhythmic pattern so that they fit to music) was made in 1565 by Thomas Sternhold. Isaac Watts (1674–1748), commonly known as the 'father of English hymnody', later made three metrical versions of the psalm, although the one that has survived in English language hymn books is a version similar to Sternhold's that was published in the 1650 Scottish Psalter. With the spelling brought up to date, this version is still sung in many Protestant churches. There is a wide choice of tunes, perhaps the best known being 'Crimond', composed around 1870 by Jessie Seymour Irvine – although when it first appeared in The Northern Psalter it was credited to David Grant, who had arranged it. But there was also 'Wiltshire' (1795) by George T. Smart, 'Martyrdom' (1800) by Hugh Wilson, 'Belmont' (1812) by William Gardner, 'Evan' (1847) by William H. Havergal, 'Orlington' by John Campbell (1807–60), and 'Brother James's Air', composed by James Leith Macbeth Bain (a man who also published his thoughts about the joys of barefoot hiking) and published in 1915.

In all of these, there is a challenge for singers. The words are written in 'common metre', and when they are sung they fall across the line in such a way that 'shepherd' and 'I'll' tend to run together. Anyone who has ever sung in a choir will, at some point, have been encouraged by their conductor not to sing 'The Lord's my shepherdile', sounding like a relative of the crocodile.

George Herbert, one of the metaphysical poets of seventeenth-century England, also adapted the psalm in his poem 'The God of Love My Shepherd Is', which is often sung as a hymn to the tune 'University'. This is not to be confused with the hymn 'The King of Love My Shepherd Is', which was written in 1868 by the Reverend Henry Baker and set to an old Irish tune.

Leonard Bernstein included a setting of Psalm 23 in the original Hebrew in his *Chichester Psalms* (1965), and the more recent setting by John Rutter will be forever associated with Dawn French's beaming smile, since it became the theme tune for *The Vicar of Dibley*.

Allegri's *Miserere*

The hauntingly beautiful *Miserere* by Allegri, which, along with Tallis's *Spem in Alium*, is one of the best examples of Renaissance polyphony, also has its origins in the book of Psalms. It is sung by two choirs standing apart from one another. The first choir sings a simple version of the original chant, and the other replies with a harmonised and ornamented version, above which floats the voice of a soprano solo, the melody rising higher and higher with each repeating strain. As a musical style it is most like falsobordone, which is a harmonised version of Gregorian chant that appeared in the late fifteenth century in southern Europe.

The *Miserere* is traditionally sung on Good Friday, the day when the death of Jesus is commemorated, and it is a song of deep repentance and sorrow for sin. The words are from the Latin version of Psalm 51 (50 in the Latin Vulgate, where the numbering is different).

This translation is from the 1662 Book of Common Prayer:

> Have mercy upon me, O God, after Thy great
>   goodness: according to the multitude of Thy
>   mercies do away mine offences.
> Wash me throughly from my wickedness: and
>   cleanse me from my sin.
> For I acknowledge my faults: and my sin is ever
>   before me.
> Against Thee only have I sinned, and done this
>   evil in thy sight: that Thou mightest be justified
>   in Thy saying, and clear when Thou art judged.
> Behold, I was shapen in wickedness: and in sin
>   hath my mother conceived me.
> But lo, Thou requirest truth in the inward parts:
>   and shalt make me to understand wisdom
>   secretly.
> Thou shalt purge me with hyssop, and I shall be
>   clean: Thou shalt wash me, and I shall be
>   whiter than snow.

By tradition, this prayer of repentance was penned by King David, Solomon's father, after one of the lowest points of his life. Although kings normally led their armies into battle, one year David sent his army out to fight while he stayed at home in Jerusalem. While they were away David caught sight of the beautiful Bathsheba, the wife of Uriah who was away with the army. David summoned Bathsheba to his palace, where he began an affair with her. When she fell pregnant, David realised that his infidelity would bring his name into dishonour, so he set about covering his tracks. Eventually he came up with a solution to his problem: he sent Uriah into the front line of battle, and after Uriah died David took Bathsheba as his own wife. Things went from bad to worse, for the child died in infancy, and David's song of lament and repentance in Psalm 51 is sorrowful almost to the point of despair. Centuries later, it was drawn into the Christian tradition and is traditionally said or sung during Holy Week, the week just before Easter, as a reflection upon the sins of the world.

Although the words of the *Miserere* come from such a sad tale, the story that lies behind the music is so fantastic that you would be forgiven for thinking it was an urban myth, but it is verified by a series of letters that were exchanged between Mozart's parents.

Settings of the *Miserere* had been composed and chanted in the Sistine Chapel since 1514. Allegri wrote his version around 1638, with some verses added in 1714 by Tommaso Bai. The *Miserere* was only sung at particular services during Holy Week, and only in the Sistine Chapel. No one was allowed to transcribe the music or sing it elsewhere, and disobeying this rule was punishable by excommunication. Although a few attempts at transcription had made their way to the royal courts of Europe, none of them were nearly as good as the original, so the rarity of the performances combined with the beauty of the setting had led to the *Miserere* being surrounded by an air of mystery.

At the age of fourteen Mozart went to Rome with his father during Holy Week. Hearing the *Miserere* for the first time, he was entranced and immediately set about writing it down from memory. Two days later he returned to the chapel to hear it again, after which he made minor corrections to his first transcription. Later on his tour, Mozart met Dr Charles Burney, a British historian, and gave him his copy, which Burney had published in London in 1771. When news of this reached the pope, he immediately sent for Mozart, who returned to Rome fearing that he was about to be excommunicated. But the pope was so impressed with Mozart's genius that all he could do was shower him with praise. The ban on the performance of the *Miserere* was then lifted, and it remains to this day one of the most popular *a cappella* choral works.

≋

The book of Psalms belongs together with four other books of wisdom – Job, Ecclesiastes, the Song of Solomon and Proverbs – and these books are the source of many common English language phrases, such as 'a two-edged sword', 'pride goes before a fall' and 'spare the rod and spoil the child'.

'Vanity of vanities', 'eat, drink and be merry' and 'there

is nothing new under the sun' come from the book of Ecclesiastes, and so do the lyrics of Pete Seeger's song 'Turn, Turn, Turn', written in 1959:

> To every thing there is a season, and a time to
> every purpose under the heaven:
> A time to be born, and a time to die; a time to
> plant, and a time to pluck up that which is
> planted;
> A time to kill, and a time to heal; a time to break
> down, and a time to build up;
> A time to weep, and a time to laugh; a time to
> mourn, and a time to dance;
> A time to cast away stones, and a time to gather
> stones together . . .
>
> (Eccl. 3:1–5 KJV)

Seeger recorded the song in 1962, and since then it has been covered by numerous other artists including Judy Collins, Joan Baez, Mary Hopkins, The Seekers, Dolly Parton, Bruce Springsteen and Belle and Sebastian. But the most enduring version is the 1965 recording by The Byrds. Roger McGuinn had arranged the song for Judy Collins, but later realised that it perfectly suited The Byrds' jangly guitar sound. When they released 'Turn, Turn, Turn' on Columbia Records in 1965 it charted on both sides of the Atlantic, but shot to the top of the charts in America, where it struck a particular chord against the background of the Vietnam War. It was later the title track for their second album. Fifty years after it was written, in May 2009,

McGuinn sang 'Turn, Turn, Turn' at Pete Seeger's ninetieth birthday party at Madison Square Gardens.

Job

Perhaps the book of wisdom that is most apt for the twenty-first century is the book of Job, the classic text about suffering that gave us the expression 'Job's comforters'. Job is catapulted in the space of a few days from a happy and comfortable life into extreme suffering. All of his children die, and then he loses his livelihood when his crops fail and his livestock perish. Then, to add insult to injury, Job himself contracts a terrible wasting disease and sits in misery scratching at his putrid skin. His wife, understandably on the verge of losing hope, coins the memorable phrase, 'Curse God and die'. And then Job's friends gather round him, but after a few days of simply sitting companionably and compassionately with Job, they begin to try to fix things for him – by engaging in a dialogue that runs through many chapters in an attempt to persuade Job that he must be suffering because he himself has done something to deserve it. Job is resolute against this pernicious idea, and eventually, at the end of the fable, God himself appears and exonerates Job.

The problem of suffering has become one of the main stumbling blocks to the acceptance of religion in contemporary society. If God is good, why would he allow innocent people to suffer? Why does God not answer prayers when people are ill, or when natural disasters happen? Does it mean that God is not there at all? Or – as C.S. Lewis once suggested – does it mean something even worse: that God does exist, but is evil and not good? A theological attempt at a theory to answer this conundrum is called a 'theodicy', but the question is not only the preserve of theologians. Novelists, psychotherapists, playwrights, musicians, poets and more have also addressed it with varying degrees of success.

In 'The Rime of the Ancient Mariner', Samuel Taylor Coleridge created a poem that sounded like an archaic folk tale about the strange journey of a ship that sails into another dimension where the sun stands still. The poem, though, is both an allegory of the inner journey of the soul and a meditation on the consequences of human failings. What was it, he wondered, that made people commit random acts of violence? And why was it that, despite the common view that suffering might be meted out by God to the wicked, it is actually endured by seemingly innocent people while those who commit crimes quite literally get away with murder? His conclusion was a mysterious mixture of guilt and grace, as the Mariner wandered through the world forgiven and restored, yet his life – which appears to go on for hundreds of years – was forever shaped by the consequences of his crime.

Half a century later, Alfred Lord Tennyson finished writing *In Memoriam*, a poem he had worked on over a long period of time, partly as a means of working out his grief over the untimely death of one of his friends, and also in response to the emerging understanding through the nineteenth century that the natural world had evolved rather than being the literal handiwork of God. As Tennyson wrote, Darwin's predecessors were already sketching out a view of the world that included a very old earth, the discovery of dinosaurs and the survival of the fittest. The rather shocking cruelty of this reality was something of an offence to the pastoral ideas of those who had grown up with a Romantic view of nature as the handwriting of God. It was Tennyson who pronounced nature 'red in tooth and claw', as he struggled to make sense of his faith against a background of personal loss, and a newly emerging understanding of the world.

Gerard Manley Hopkins's poem 'The Wreck of the Deutschland', also about the journey of a ship, is a long poem that explores the subject of suffering. Although not published until 1918, the poem was written in 1875–6 in response to a real disaster. In December 1875 the SS *Deutschland*, which had been thought unsinkable, was carrying hopeful emigrants to a new life in America when it was shipwrecked off the east coast of England. Any shipwreck is tragic, but this one seemed to Hopkins to symbolise a more metaphysical disaster, for the prevailing mood of the time was one of heightened optimism concerning human progress. It almost seemed to Hopkins that the shipwreck was a portent of a greater human disaster. Among those who died were five Franciscan nuns who had been bound for New York, emigrating to escape the anti-Catholic laws in their home country and looking towards a life where their faith could be freely expressed. To Hopkins, this added a particular misery to the disaster, in that a seeming act of faith in God had ended in such a cruel manner. Like Tennyson, Hopkins struggled with the fact that God was clearly not in direct control of nature, but, taking the five nuns as emblematic of the five wounds of Christ, he worked through the problem of suffering by envisaging God as being within the suffering, rather than as a cosmic power that failed to notice or care about the state of humanity. In this, Hopkins prefigured much of the theology that followed in the twentieth century, which focused less on God as the controller of the elements and more on a God who suffers alongside and within humanity.

It is frustrating to the modern reader, who expects a reasoned answer to every question, that when God appears at the end of Job, he does not give a satisfactory answer as to the cause of Job's suffering. But the greatest legacy of the book of Job is its challenge to the age-old, enslaving idea that people bring their suffering on themselves. Job affirms that sometimes suffering happens, not because of sin or misdeeds or bad karma, but just because it does. When Job was written in its present form, probably in the fifth or sixth century BC, it was absolutely revolutionary to suggest that suffering was bad luck and not punishment, but even now there is not a complete absence of condemnation when people suffer a run of bad luck: it seems to be a human tendency to suspect that somehow people are bringing their suffering on themselves.

Job's tragic-comic story has inspired all kinds of art and literature. William Blake made a series of drawings of Job and his wife and friends, which are now in the Tate Collection, and in 1928, a hundred years after Blake's death, Geoffrey Keynes, a Blake scholar and a ballet enthusiast, took these sketches as the inspiration for a new ballet. Vaughan Williams was drawn in to compose the music, which he entitled *Job, A Masque for Dancing*. As it turned out, the ballet was not a success (perhaps unsurprising, since most of the narrative involves four men sitting down and talking!), but Vaughan Williams's music was a master-piece, drawing together his penchant for pastoral folk tunes and the huge, symphonic landscapes more typical of his later work.

6
Writing on the wall

Have you ever been told that 'a leopard can't change his spots', or had your 'teeth set on edge' by someone scraping their fingernails down a blackboard? These expressions come from the writings of the Old Testament prophets, along with a whole host of everyday phrases: 'the writing's on the wall'; 'he has feet of clay'; 'they don't see eye to eye'; 'there are wheels within wheels'; 'it's a drop in the bucket'; 'white as snow'; 'holier than thou' . . .

A prophet is popularly thought of as someone who predicts the future, like a soothsayer or divine fortune-teller. But while they did talk about the future, and claimed to be speaking on behalf of God, the Old Testament prophets were not fortune-tellers but truth-tellers – people who, with the aid of divine revelation, could read the signs of the times, seeing through political spin to read the motives and morals that lay beneath the surface. They pointed out where the state of the nation had come adrift from the ideals laid down in their codes and laws, and called on people to smarten up their behaviour. Their words were as much about social justice, financial honesty and personal humility as religion, and although they sometimes predicted dire consequences, they also gave their hearers a choice, making it clear that people could change the outcome of events if they heeded the warnings. Whereas fortune-tellers needed to get their predictions right, for a prophet the best possible outcome would often be that people would heed their words and avoid the prophecy being fulfilled.

Prophets crop up all the way through the Bible, and the early ones often banded together in 'schools'. Some of them were known as 'shouters' who indulged in ecstatic worship, and some were principal advisors to Israel's monarchs. We have already encountered Nathan the prophet, King David's advisor who was present at Solomon's coronation. But the greatest of the early prophets was Elijah, whose adventures have been the inspiration for all kinds of later writing and art and folk ideas.[1] Elijah predicted drought and famine, which he believed were a judgement from God. He also worked various miracles, such as making a poor widow's kitchen supplies never run out, and consistently preached against monarchs who looked after their own interests but failed the people. Unsurprisingly this did not increase his popularity with the fat-cat kings and queens, and Elijah hit a low point when his life was threatened by the wicked Queen Jezebel, the epitome of all that was cruel and perverse. Elijah deserted his post and ran for his life to a remote desert cave, where he sat feeling sorry for himself and waited to hear God's voice. There followed a series of dramatic incidents that would seem a suitable accompaniment to a divine utterance – an earthquake, a huge storm and a fire. But through all this commotion God was silent, and when he eventually did speak, it was in an almost inaudible whisper – a mere movement of breath. Silence and stillness lie at the heart of the Quaker movement, and as Quaker ritual does not involve singing, it is something of a rarity to find a hymn written by a Quaker. 'Dear Lord and Father of Mankind' was originally the conclusion of a long poem, 'The Brewing of Soma', by American Quaker poet John Greenleaf Whittier, and expresses the Quaker ideal of prayer, which is to contemplate in silence in order to hear the 'still small voice' of 1 Kings 19:11–13. In the UK the hymn is sung to the tune 'Repton' by Hubert Parry, who also wrote 'Jerusalem', while Frederick Charles Maker's tune 'Rest' is more familiar in the USA. The hymn reflects on various moments of quietness in the life of Jesus, but ends with a reference to Elijah's night in the desert cave: 'Breathe through the earthquake, wind and fire, O still small voice of Calm.' As well as consistently topping lists of Britain's favourite hymns, 'Dear Lord and Father' was also part of the soundtrack to the 2007 film *Atonement*, where it is played during the scene of the Dunkirk evacuation.

The later prophets, who lived between about 850 and 350 BC, were known less for their exploits than for their words, recorded in books which, with two exceptions, were named after their authors (although, truth be told, there were probably other people involved in the writing process – ghostwriting is not a new skill!). The books of the prophets are full of comedy and tragedy, fantasy adventures, tales of heroism, mystical poetry and graphic imagination, and their words – or corruptions of them – are threaded all the way through our language. These prophets are divided into two groups – the major prophets, Isaiah, Jeremiah (who also wrote the book of Lamentations), Ezekiel and Daniel, and then twelve who wrote shorter books known as the 'minor prophets'. Their dates and contexts vary. Some came from the northern kingdom and some from the south, and their messages have different emphases – some are practical and others mystical, some are interested in politics and others more specifically concerned with religious issues. In their original context the common thread between all of them was their role in guiding the nation, while later on in Christian thought their chief significance was the foretelling of salvation through Jesus Christ, the Messiah.

Some of the curiosities seen in art galleries trace their source back to the prophets – one example being Fra Angelico's *Ezekiel's Vision of the Mystic Wheel* (c. 1450, Museo di San Marco, Florence, Italy), which is described in Ezekiel 1:15–18. Ezekiel was given to a genre in the realm of symbolic fantasy, speaking of extraordinary creatures that easily rival those in *Lord of the Rings* or *Harry Potter*, and geometric shapes that seem full of meaning, although for the modern reader the interpretation is largely down to guesswork.

Portraits of the prophets themselves also appear in a number of places, again with symbolic meaning. In the Sistine Chapel, Michelangelo placed seven Old Testament prophets alongside five Greek female Sibyls, who together represent the coming of Christ. The pagan figures, alternated with Jeremiah, Ezekiel, Isaiah, Joel and Daniel, are there to show that the Messiah came not only for the Jewish world but to bring a universal message of redemption, and in addition that the Judaic revelation of Christ can be seen as congruent with the revelations of the classical world. Two other prophets have symbolic positions in the Sistine Chapel. Zechariah, who is considered to be the main prophet of the passion of Christ, appears above the chapel door through which the pope processes on Palm Sunday – the day on which Christ entered into Jerusalem at the beginning of the week of his passion (the days leading up to his death). And over the altar is Jonah, one of the most colourful of the minor prophets, popularly remembered as having been thrown overboard in a storm and swallowed by a whale (although the Bible actually says a large fish). Jonah's story has its serious side, but it is also full of comedy. It begins with Jonah being told by God to go and preach to the city of Nineveh, calling them to mend their ways or their city and their lifestyle will implode. Jonah, however, decides to make a run for it and boards a ship sailing in the opposite direction. God sends a storm and Jonah is thrown overboard, at which point the big fish swallows him. Jonah is spewed up onto the beach three days later, caves in to God's calling and goes to Nineveh and preaches hell-fire and damnation. The people of Nineveh, though, are impressed by Jonah's message and change their ways, as a result of which their city is not destroyed – illustrating perfectly the fact that a prophet is not a fortune-teller. The comedy is complete when Jonah then goes off and sulks, saying to God, 'I knew it! I knew you would be merciful; that's why I didn't want to go there in the first place!'

Another way to read Jonah is to give it a psychological and political reading, which suggests that religion is useless if it is purely an interior exercise – something self-centred and disconnected from real life. It is valid only if it functions within society to bring about justice and peace. The ancient author expresses outrage at the fat-cat aspects of city life, and calls Jonah to do something about it. The fish's belly becomes a metaphor for the rottenness of a self-indulgent religion, and the city represents the affairs of the world as the true location and motivation for faith.

Jonah's portrait appears in Tissot's series on the prophets, in the Tate (*Jonah and the Whale*, 1967, Arpad Illes), the Smithsonian (*Jonah at Sea*, c. 1885–95, Albert Pinkham Ryder) and the National Maritime Museum (*Jonah and the Whale*, c. 1610–20, Adam Willaerts), and his name has inspired bands, songs and album titles (from *Jonah and the Whale* to *Jonah Ate the Whale*). But the reason his portrait appears above the altar in the Sistine Chapel is that he has become known as the prophet of the resurrection. His surviving a three-day 'death' in the belly of the fish is seen as prophetic of Jesus dying, being laid in a tomb and being resurrected on the third day. Perhaps Jonah would have cheered up if he had known that his misfortunes would take on this prophetic significance.

Isaiah

A common English pub name, The Lion and Lamb, is also the nickname of a rocky outcrop near Grasmere in the Lake District, and a phrase associated with various peacemaking projects, songs and poems. Individually these two animals have symbolic meaning within Christianity. The lion represents the resurrection, as C.S. Lewis knew when he chose Aslan as his death-defying Narnian hero, and the lamb symbolises Jesus as Redeemer. But the unlikely combination of the lion and the lamb finds its origin in the poetic imagery of Isaiah. 'The lion shall lie down with the lamb' is a popular reduction of his vision of peace:

The wolf will live with the lamb,
the leopard will lie down with the goat,
the calf and the lion and the yearling together,
and a little child will lead them.
The cow will feed with the bear,
their young will lie down together,
and the lion will eat straw like the ox.
Infants will play near the hole of the cobra;
young children will put their hands into the viper's
    nest.
They will neither harm nor destroy
on all my holy mountain,
for the earth will be filled with the knowledge of the
    LORD
as the waters cover the sea.

(Isa. 11:6–9)

This prophecy has often been treated as a kind of 'neverland' view of heaven, a promise for the world to come, but something that can never be achieved in the world in which we live. But there are plenty who have taken Isaiah's imagery as a gritty aspiration towards making a real political peace. American singer-songwriter Steve Earle borrowed Isaiah's words in a song of hope for political peace. Among a collection of rather fatalistic songs in response to 9/11, the title song of his 2002 album *Jerusalem* declares his belief, seemingly against the odds, that one day the lion and the lamb really will lie down together, not only in a metaphysical dimension, but in the real world.[2]

Others before now have also taken Isaiah's vision as aspirational, rather than dismissing it as pie in the sky. American painter Edward Hicks (1780–1849) made a series of sixty paintings on the theme of the Peaceable Kingdom – one example of which is in the National Gallery of Art, Washington DC. Hicks relocated Isaiah's vision to the woods of Pennsylvania. In the foreground he shows some small children, based on portraits of his own children, playing happily among the incongruous collection of jungle and farmyard animals from Isaiah's prophecy. Animals that would normally eat each other are seen grazing together, a lamb lies at the foot of a surprisingly tame and unhungry lion, while the children pull the lion's mane and pat the leopard's nose. In the background a group of Native Americans and Quakers are gathered around William Penn as he makes a land treaty with the Delaware Indians. At a time when many settlers claimed land without payment, Penn was renowned among the colonists for being (by the standards of his time, at least) the most just in his dealings with the Native Americans, settling on them considerable sums of money. Penn's commitment to peace and justice grew out of his Quaker principles, and Edward Hicks, who was also a Quaker, viewed Penn's political act as an outworking of Isaiah's vision of justice and peace.

The Tree of Jesse

There is a recurring image in religious art, especially in stained glass and medieval illuminations, of a tree with a whole crowd of people sitting in its branches. It is known as the Jesse Tree, and it is a kind of family tree that traces the genealogy of Jesus back to Jesse, King David's father. But unlike a genealogy chart, the most ancient ancestor is at the bottom, not the top of the picture, and the characters appear not just as names, but as figures perched in the branches of a tree. Most depictions of the Jesse Tree show Jesse himself reclining or sleeping at the foot of the picture, with a tree growing out of his ribcage. Jesse often appears proportionately larger than the other figures. The branches spread out to each side, and all the ancestors of Jesus stand or sit in the branches, while the trunk of the tree stretches vertically to the top of the picture where Mary sits with Jesus, who must be at the top to show his superiority. Many people believe that the Jesse Tree is the origin of the tradition of the Christmas tree.

Jesse was of particular significance in the Old Testament because he was the father of King David and the ancestor of Jesus. The Jesse Tree became one of the chief representations of the prophets in Christian art, because the announcement of a coming Messiah or Saviour was one of the central threads of their message. For many centuries the perception of the prophets' words as a prediction of the life and work of Jesus completely eclipsed any interest in what meaning they had in their original context. The Jesse Tree tradition was based on words from Isaiah, who is not only the most verbose of the prophets, but also the most-quoted in the later books of the Bible:

> A shoot will come up from the stump of Jesse;
> from his roots a Branch will bear fruit.
>
> (Isa. 11:1)

Much later Jesus was claimed by the early Christians as the Messiah, and Matthew took a lot of trouble to begin his Gospel with a complete genealogy of Jesus to demonstrate Jesus' credentials as the true Messiah (Matt. 1:1–17). Beginning with Abraham, Matthew traced the line of descent through Jesse and King David to Joseph, the husband of Mary the mother of Jesus. Given that it is Joseph who completes the genealogical line from Jesse to Jesus, it is interesting to see that Mary is always with Jesus at the top of the Jesse Tree, while Joseph sometimes does not appear at all. When St Jerome translated the Bible into Latin in the fifth century, he chose the Latin word *virgo* to render the Hebrew word for 'twig' or 'rod' in Isaiah's prophecy, and then added the words *virga est virgo* – 'the twig is the Virgin'.[3] Thus it was that the Jesse Tree touched the nerve of medieval Marianism, and was at the height of its popularity in medieval art.

The Jesse Tree is often found as an illustration of Matthew's Gospel as he shows the fulfilment of Isaiah's prophecy, the earliest known picture of a Jesse Tree being in a late eleventh-century Gospel book in Prague.[4] But the Jesse Tree was even more common in English medieval Psalters (books of psalms), where it was commonly painted on the first page. The Psalms were connected to the fulfilment of Isaiah's prophecy because, by tradition, they were thought to have been written by King David, Jesse's son. But Psalm 1 is also a song about a tree, and as luck would have it, it begins with the word 'Blessed' (*Beatus* in Latin), a capital B being the perfect shape for illuminating with the shape of the tree.

Blessed is the man
who does not walk in the counsel of the wicked
or stand in the way of sinners
or sit in the seat of mockers.
But his delight is in the law of the LORD,
and on his law he meditates day and night.
He is like a tree planted by streams of water,
which yields its fruit in season
and whose leaf does not wither.

(Ps. 1:1–3 NIV)

In 2004, the Earl of Macclesfield was clearing out his library in Oxfordshire, and he came across an old Psalter. There within its pages was a very elaborate Jesse Tree, with the branches extending beyond the capital B all the way round the sides and lower edge of the text.[5] The Macclesfield Psalter was dated to 1330, and was quickly identified as being by the same artist who illustrated the Gorleston Psalter, which dates from somewhere between 1310 and 1325 and is in the British Library. The artist's name is unknown, but he was a Franciscan friar from St Andrew's Church in Gorleston, Great Yarmouth, and is considered to be one of the greatest English medieval artists. The Macclesfield Psalter almost ended up in California after being auctioned at Sotheby's, but a national campaign to keep it close to its East Anglian origins led to it being kept in the Fitzwilliam Museum in Cambridge.

The Jesse Tree appears in a number of stained-glass windows, the oldest complete one being in Chartres Cathedral in France, dating back to 1140–50. There are two early Jesse Tree fragments in England: one in York Minster is thought to be the oldest example of stained glass in England, and there is another in Canterbury Cathedral. Later examples are plentiful, but there is a particularly wonderful one at the church of Saint-Etienne in Beauvais, France, which shows Jesse lying not in his usual position on the ground, but in the comfort of a magnificent four-poster bed.

The Rijksmuseum in Amsterdam has a painting of the Tree of Jesse from around 1490 or 1500, attributed to Geertgen tot Sint Jans. It shows Jesus' ancestors in much the same pattern as other Jesse Trees, neatly dressed in fifteenth-century Dutch costume. But unlike the stylised figures in stained glass or manuscript illuminations, Geertgen's painting makes the figures more realistic, creating a somewhat comic effect as they stand or crouch in the branches of the tree. King David is easily identifiable by his harp and crown, and on the next branch sits Solomon in striped leggings. The remaining figures – only a selection of the whole list – include a youthful version of King Rehoboam hoisting an aged descendant up onto the next branch, as the poor old chap clearly cannot manage the climb by himself. The background to Geertgen's painting is unusual too: Jesse is asleep in a walled courtyard, a metaphor for Mary's virginity that has its origins in the Song of Solomon. Around the foot of the tree are three figures. On the right stands a distinguished ecclesiastical figure who appears to be reading from the Bible – probably the prophecy from Isaiah 11:1–3. Until 1932, on the left of the picture was a garden wall, but when the painting was restored it was discovered that, for reasons that are not clear, the garden wall had been extended to paint out two earlier figures – a kneeling nun dressed in white and a pilgrim with a flowing white beard who may be Isaiah himself.

Jesse Trees are also found in the floors, ceilings and stonework of ecclesiastical buildings. The wooden nave ceiling at Ely Cathedral is a complete painted Jesse Tree, which was begun by Henry Le Strange in 1858 and completed seven years later by Thomas Gambier Parry, a friend of Le Strange and the father of composer Sir Hubert Parry. The two artists painted the ceiling *in situ*, lying on their backs on scaffolding like Michelangelo. A twentieth-century Jesse Tree appears in the marble mosaic floor of the Lady Chapel at the Abbey Church, Buckfast Abbey, Devon.

Jeremiah

Jeremiah reads as though he was somewhat melancholic by nature. He was given to rather dramatic symbolic actions. Once he bought a brand-new pair of underpants, buried them by the river bank and then dug them up a week later and showed everyone that they had rotted. This was intended as a metaphor for the way Israel had disconnected from God. The idea was that your clothes are supposed to stay next to your skin, but if they are left out in the rain they go mouldy. Similarly the people were meant to stay intimately connected to their God, so by giving no thought to God they would, in effect, become mouldy and useless. Jeremiah lived up to the caricature of a 'prophet of doom'. He spent several years sounding a series of warnings that if people did not turn back to God their city would fall to their enemies. He pleaded with them that if they did not wake up to their situation the cost in human life would be unimaginable.

Eventually Jerusalem was destroyed just as the prophets had warned, the ruling classes were taken into exile, and the

poor were left in their ruined land to fend for themselves.
Jeremiah wrote a second book called Lamentations – a heart-
breakingly sad and poignant poem about the destruction of
his beloved city:

> 'I called to my allies
> but they betrayed me.
> My priests and my elders
> perished in the city
> while they searched for food
> to keep themselves alive . . .
> 'People have heard my groaning,
> but there is no-one to comfort me.
> All my enemies have heard of my distress;
> they rejoice at what you have done.
> May you bring the day you have announced
> so they may become like me.'
>
> (Lam. 1:19, 21)

The overwhelming grief expressed in Lamentations, accom-
panied by the complete absence of anyone to help, is echoed
in Siegfried Sassoon's poem 'Lamentations'. The biblical
allusion of Sassoon's title highlights his own belief that the
devastation of human life at the front was completely overlooked by the commanders of the First World War who, in
his view, were focused on the objective of an unwinnable war
at shocking human expense:

> I found him in the guard-room at the Base.
> From the blind darkness I had heard his crying
> And blundered in. With puzzled, patient face

A sergeant watched him; it was no good trying
To stop it; for he howled and beat his chest.
And, all because his brother had gone west,
Raved at the bleeding war; his rampant grief
Moaned, shouted, sobbed, and choked, while he was
    kneeling
Half-naked on the floor. In my belief
Such men have lost all patriotic feeling.[6]

Rembrandt captured the heavy-hearted prophet in *Jeremiah Lamenting the Destruction of Jerusalem* (1630, Rijksmuseum, Amsterdam), but as the old man sits desolate, with the glow of the burning city behind him, he still retains the prophetic quality that always looks forward into the future. In the middle of his bleak poem, Jeremiah writes:

Yet this I call to mind
and therefore I have hope:
Because of the LORD's great love we are not
    consumed,
for his compassions never fail.
They are new every morning;
great is your faithfulness.
I say to myself, 'The LORD is my portion;
therefore I will wait for him.'
The LORD is good to those whose hope is in him,
to the one who seeks him;
it is good to wait quietly
for the salvation of the LORD.

                  (Lam. 3:21–6)

In essence, despite his melancholic tendencies, Jeremiah is convinced that while there is life, there is hope – and the elegant construction of Lamentations adds to the sense that it is ultimately a song of hope, not despair. The whole of the first chapter is an acrostic poem – the verses beginning with each letter of the Hebrew alphabet in order. So it is not just an undigested outpouring of grief, it is a work of art in which Jeremiah is rebuilding order out of the rubble of destruction. Poetry and art, like the most authentic kinds of spirituality, are often expressive of the drive to create order out of chaos, and Lamentations is a classic example of this.

Daniel

The book of Daniel, rather than being written by the prophet himself, seems to have been written later as a work of historical fiction. It is set in Babylon during the time of the exile, and – with a few elaborations – is apparently about a real person, but it reads like a dramatic movie script, lurching from one extraordinary event to another, which is probably why Daniel features more often than the other prophets in music, art and literature.

Many of the details of the book of Daniel tie up with sources discovered in ancient Babylon, but they each spin the story to their own advantage. The Babylonian writers laud their great kings as heroes of immense dignity and success and gloss over their failings, while the biblical accounts put the spotlight on the supremacy of their own God and make a meal of their captors' weaknesses. So Nebuchadnezzar, who was immensely powerful and a legendary figure in his own land, appears in Daniel to disadvantage and as no match for the true God.

Those who were carried off to Babylon in 586 BC were mostly the Jewish nobility, and Daniel was chosen to enter Nebuchadnezzar's service in the royal court, while three of his friends, who had been given the Babylonian names Shadrach, Meshach and Abednego, were given high-ranking civil service jobs. But they were determined not to be completely subsumed into Babylonian culture and remained loyal to their Jewish identity. Before long, an immense statue of Nebuchadnezzar was erected and everyone was ordered to bow down and worship it. Shadrach, Meshach and Abednego refused to obey the king's command and were punished by being thrown to their deaths in a fiercely hot furnace. Miraculously, though, they survived and walked away unharmed. One illustration of this is *The Three Hebrews in the Fiery Furnace*, painted by Pieter Aertsen (c. 1552, Museum Boijmans Van Beuningen, Rotterdam).

If Nebuchadnezzar was such a great king, why does William Blake's copperplate illustration *Nebuchadnezzar* (1795) show him as a dishevelled figure with wild eyes and claw-like nails, crawling on all fours? According to the biblical account, Nebuchadnezzar had a strange dream which Daniel interpreted. He told the king that unless he renounced his pride and acknowledged God, he would lose his authority and be condemned to live like an animal for seven years. Nebuchadnezzar did not heed the warning and before long he found himself reduced to a shadow of his former self:

Nebuchadnezzar . . . was driven away from people and ate grass like the ox. His body was drenched with the

> dew of heaven until his hair grew like the feathers of
> an eagle and his nails like the claws of a bird.
>
> (Dan. 4:33)

Babylonian sources, though, suggest that it was Nabonidus, Nebuchadnezzar's son, who endured a period of mental illness, and it seems likely that the biblical account has combined the two stories. Nabonidus left Babylon in the care of his son Belshazzar for eleven years while he pursued an ill-fated campaign to gain control of various trade routes. Belshazzar proved a poor regent, and the downfall of Babylon that followed is the next episode in Daniel's story. Belshazzar held a great feast, and he and his wives began to drink wine from the goblets that had been brought from the temple in Jerusalem – an act that was seen as desecration by the Israelites. Then a mysterious, disembodied hand began to write on the wall.

> In the same hour came forth fingers of a man's hand,
> and wrote over against the candlestick upon the
> plaister of the wall of the king's palace: and the king
> saw the part of the hand that wrote. Then the king's
> countenance was changed, and his thoughts troubled
> him, so that the joints of his loins were loosed, and
> his knees smote one against another. The king cried
> aloud to bring in the astrologers, the Chaldeans, and
> the soothsayers . . .
>
> (Dan. 5:5–7 KJV)

At first no one knew what it meant, and Belshazzar was so terrified his knees were knocking. He promised power and riches to anyone who could interpret the mysterious writing. Daniel was summoned, and he told Belshazzar that he had profaned the temple vessels and that the writing on the wall was a message in Aramaic: *mene, mene, tekel, upharsin*. This is a corruption of the names of coins: a *pharsin* is two *pheres*, which make a *tekel*, and sixty *tekels* make a *mene*. The five coins (two *menes*, one *tekel*, two *pheres*), mentioned in descending order of value, could be seen to represent Nebuchadnezzar's successors and the gradual decline of the kingdom. But the three names of the coins also resemble three Aramaic verbs: 'numbered, weighed, and divided', and this makes sense of Daniel's interpretation of the message:

> This is what these words mean:
> *Mene*: God has numbered the days of your reign
> and brought it to an end.
> *Tekel*: You have been weighed on the scales and
> found wanting.
> *Peres*: Your kingdom is divided and given to the
> Medes and Persians.
>
> (Dan. 5:26–8)

Sure enough, Belshazzar died the very same night, and Babylon was conquered and (according to the biblical account) divided between Darius of the Medes and Cyrus the Persian king. Other historical evidence confirms Cyrus as the Persian king who conquered Babylon, while it is less clear where Darius and the Medes fit into the picture. But later Daniel quotes the 'law of the Medes and the Persians' as a rule that it is impossible to break – again a phrase that became common in English usage.

Belshazzar's Feast, an oratorio by English composer William Walton, with libretto by Osbert Sitwell, was first performed at the Leeds Festival on 8 October 1931 and remains one of Walton's best-known compositions and one of the most popular works in the English choral repertoire. Engravings were made for editions of the Bible by such renowned illustrators as Matthias Scheits and Gustave Dore. Rembrandt painted Belshazzar's feast in 1635, and it was also an irresistible subject for English painter John Martin, who painted it under the same title in 1820/1.

The writing on the wall has also been adapted to illustrate other situations of impending judgement or doom. Jonathan Swift, in his poem 'The Run upon the Bankers', applied the image to the banking profession:

> A baited banker thus desponds,
> From his own hand foresees his fall,
> They have his soul, who have his bonds;
> 'Tis like the writing on the wall.

Belshazzar's feast also gave us the phrase 'to be weighed in the balance', a metaphor for judgement that dates back at least as far as the fourteenth century in English. British caricaturist James Gillray (1757–1815) used both images in his cartoon entitled *Napoleon is About to Make a Meal of England When Writing on the Wall Warns Him to Think Again*. Two arms appear through the clouds, one writing the doom-laden words on the wall and the other holding a pair of legal scales. Beneath them, Napoleon sits with some soldiers and women, and an immensely fat Josephine, feasting at a table. In addition to food on the table, there are dishes with miniatures of the Bank of England, St James, the Tower of London and 'Roast Beef of Old England'. Napoleon himself, though, turns in horror to see the hand writing on the wall.

Historical and archaeological finds have shown that it was not hard for Cyrus the Great to conquer Babylonia. The great empire had been resting on its laurels since the rule of Nebuchadnezzar, and while Nabonidus was off on his travels, Belshazzar had proved ineffectual as commander of the army. Meantime, Cyrus had gradually been building up his empire. Immediately after the doom-laden feast, Belshazzar gathered his troops to defend a city on the Persian-Babylonian border where he was killed and Cyrus became the victor in an otherwise bloodless conquest. Why the Babylonian armies did not fight harder is unclear, although it may be that they knew they were in decline and were ready to welcome the powerful and sophisticated culture of Persia. In any event, Babylon was taken by Cyrus on 12 October 539 BC and under his rule Babylon again became a great city, famous not only for wealth and power, but also for its advances in science. Priest-scholars studied the heavens and drew maps of the constellations that were foundational for modern astronomy and mathematics. Our clocks, measuring time in units of twelve, five and sixty, have their origins in Babylonian mathematics.

It is not immediately obvious as you read through Daniel that there are long lapses of time between the dramatic events of his life. In fact, several decades must have gone by between the chapters, and he must have been quite elderly by the time the Persians ruled Babylon. Under Persian rule, Daniel was again given a high position as a chief minister, but his popularity with the king did not go down too well with the other courtiers and they plotted to get rid of him by tricking the king into throwing Daniel into a den of lions.

At the first light of dawn, the king got up and hurried to the lions' den. When he came near the den, he called to Daniel in an anguished voice, 'Daniel, servant of the living God, has your God, whom you serve continually, been able to rescue you from the lions?'

Daniel answered, 'May the king live forever! My God sent his angel, and he shut the mouths of the lions. They have not hurt me, because I was found innocent in his sight. Nor have I ever done any wrong before you, Your Majesty.'

The king was overjoyed and gave orders to lift Daniel out of the den. And when Daniel was lifted from the den, no wound was found on him, because he had trusted in his God.

(Dan. 6:19–23)

Rembrandt, Rubens, Jan Brueghel the Younger and English painter Briton Riviere are among many artists who produced works entitled *Daniel in the Lions' Den*, most of which show Daniel as a youth, looking up to heaven for the help of his God.

Three years into Cyrus's reign, he allowed the Jews to return to Jerusalem. By that time Daniel was a very old man – perhaps a hundred years old – and he remained in Babylon until his death. Tradition has it that he died at Susa, in modern-day Iran, where his tomb is at a site known as Shush-e Daniyal. But as with many such ancient figures, the burial place is disputed, and there are also burial sites in ancient Babylon and in Kirkuk, Iraq. Babylon itself was conquered again in 331 BC by Alexander the Great, but by 130 BC, when the Parthian empire had conquered most of the Near East, the writing really was on the wall for the ancient city. After one last invasion it fell into ruins and lay buried in the sands of time for two millennia before being rediscovered by archaeologists.

＝

We have seen through this chapter that the prophets addressed their own time and culture, and that their words were later reinterpreted. In particular they have been read in Christian theology as foretelling the coming of Jesus Christ as the Messiah, and that will be the subject of the next chapter.

7
Messiah

Handel's *Messiah* is one of the most popular choral works of all time. Handel composed it at amazing speed, completing the entire score in less than a month, and he had a dramatic religious epiphany as he wrote it. The source of his mystical experience is a matter of debate. Some say that the adrenaline and sleeplessness of his punishing schedule induced a euphoric state, while others have suggested that he might have been using various substances to keep himself awake and these produced his mystical feelings. Others believe that the power of the ancient words affected him so profoundly that he really did have a spiritual epiphany. Whatever the truth behind the story, Handel himself believed in his own experience and continued from that time on in a deeper religious devotion.

On 17 April 1742 the *Dublin Journal* said in its review of the first performance, 'Words are wanting to express the exquisite Delight it afforded to the admiring crouded Audience. The Sublime, the Grand, and the Tender, adapted to the most elevated, majestick and moving Words composed to transport and charm the ravished Heart and Ear.'

Unsurprisingly, Handel immediately made plans for further performances in Dublin, but on 23 March the following year it was performed at Covent Garden in London, and this time some controversy followed, mostly due to the fact that a religious work was being performed by theatrical singers in a secular venue. Nowadays that would seem unremarkable: churches and cathedrals frequently host secular concerts while church groups meet in coffee houses, homes and disused theatres. But in the eighteenth century the theatre was seen as distinctly in contrast to spiritual concerns, and the performance of *Messiah* in a theatre, sung by entertainers not church musicians, seemed to many an insult to the sacred content. Regardless of who performed it, however, *Messiah* had a huge impact, and after going through various versions became established in the English repertoire.

Messiah was written in three parts, opening with Isaiah's prophecy of the coming Messiah and the angels' announce-ments of Christ's birth. Part Two is about the redemption achieved through the sacrifice of Jesus and the futility of human opposition to that redemption. Part Three is a declar-ation of the hope of eternal life through Christ. Even in his own lifetime Handel rearranged and rewrote sections of it for particular performances. But the work is nowadays rarely heard in its entirety, and although it was originally written to be sung in Holy Week, the week before Easter, the parts which meditate on Christ's death are now usually omitted and the shorter version is firmly associated with Christmas.

The libretto was penned by Charles Jennens, an English landowner and patron of the arts. He was no great literary talent, but he had the ability to assemble the biblical texts to dramatic effect, and he produced libretti for four more of

Handel's oratorios, one of which was drawn from poems by John Milton, and three from dramatic Old Testament stories – *Saul, Israel in Egypt* and *Belshazzar*. Unlike these, though, *Messiah* does not have a plot line as such. Jennens only drew minimally from the Gospels, and instead produced a libretto based chiefly on the words of the prophets Isaiah, Zechariah, Malachi and Haggai, and from the book of Job, the Psalms and Lamentations. The result was not so much a narrative of Jesus' birth, life and death as a meditation on the theological significance of the Messiah, and it is a clear demonstration of the extent to which the prophets' words were reappropriated as a foretelling of Jesus Christ – which, if they could have seen that far into the future, would probably have amazed them.

The name 'Messiah' is traced back in English to about 1300. It came to us via Latin and Greek, and before that from Aramaic *meshiha* and Hebrew *mashiah*, which means 'anointed of the Lord'. In the Greek Septuagint translation this is rendered as *Khristos*, from which we get the word 'Christ'. In Old Testament prophecy, various words were used to describe someone who would come as deliverer of the Jewish nation, who would release them from exile and restore them to their homeland. The Messianic hope continued to develop both as a spiritual and political idea, and in Jesus' time included the hope of deliverance from Roman occupation. Mark's Gospel suggests that Jesus' followers gradually began to identify him as the Messiah, but then had to change their understanding of what that might mean – a crucified Messiah was not at all what they were expecting. By the time the earliest New Testament documents were written down, the writers had made the adjustment to a

Messiah concerned less with worldly empires than with the spiritual realm.

Fast-forward to the eighteenth century, and what kind of Messiah emerges when Jennens takes the Old Testament messianic prophecies, mixes them with the story of Jesus, and Handel sets them to music? Among the Old Testament metaphors that he chose were a suffering servant, a shepherd, a redeemer and a king. *Messiah* begins with these words:

> Comfort ye, comfort ye my people, saith your God.
> Speak ye comfortably to Jerusalem, and cry unto
>   her, that her warfare is accomplished, that her
>   iniquity is pardoned.
> The voice of him that crieth in the wilderness;
>   prepare ye the way of the Lord; make straight in
>   the desert a highway for our God.
>
> (From Isa. 40:1–3 KJV)

'Comfort ye my people' is the opening of *Messiah*, but it is also the beginning of a completely new section in Isaiah's book. It is such a noticeable change of tone that years after Jennens and Handel were playing with the words, scholars began to wonder whether Isaiah's prophecies had been written by two or even three authors, either side of the exile. But Jennens was concerned only with showing that the Messiah predicted by the prophets was ultimately fulfilled in Jesus.

Isaiah's words 'Comfort ye' – both in their original context and adopted into Christian thought – are not a message of sympathy. We use the word 'comfort' in contexts like comfort

blanket or comfort food – something to pamper yourself
with and make you feel better when things are tough. But in
this context, 'comfort' suggests a kind of motivational
strengthening: not so much 'stay indoors and have a duvet
day' as 'come on, get up and get ready; things are about to
happen'. It is a proclamation that things can only get better.

But what about the 'voice crying in the wilderness'? Today
we use that phrase to mean 'a warning that no one heeds'.
But the original Hebrew did not really mean that. A more
accurate translation is:

> A voice cries out:
> 'In the wilderness prepare the way of the LORD,
> make straight in the desert a highway for our God.'
> (Isa. 40:3 NRSV)

It is a subtle but important difference, showing that it really
does matter where you put the comma! Isaiah was not talking about a voice crying in the wilderness, but a voice crying
out, 'Make a way through the wilderness.' But the translation
from Hebrew to Greek, and from Greek to Latin to King
James English, established the image of the lone voice in
the desert. And it was helped along by Matthew's Gospel,
which applied Isaiah's words to John the Baptist:

> This is the one of whom the prophet Isaiah spoke
>   when he said,
> 'The voice of one crying out in the wilderness:
> "Prepare the way of the Lord,
> make his paths straight."'
> (Matt. 3:3 NRSV)

The image of John the Baptist living like a hermit in the desert and calling out his message hoping someone would hear became lodged deep in Christian thought, but in their original context Isaiah's words concerned the returning exiles.

The rebuilding of Jerusalem is recorded at length in the books of Ezra and Nehemiah. But the return itself meant a long journey through the desert – which for the exiles, who had faithfully kept alive the memory of their escape from Egypt, would have surely given them a sense of *déjà vu*. Isaiah's message was one of hope that unlike the circuitous desert wanderings of the Exodus, this return would be swift and efficient, on a highway through the desert. But despite the realisation that Isaiah was talking about an actual journey, the phrase 'a voice crying in the wilderness' had become so firmly lodged in the English language that no modern-day voice crying in the wilderness is likely to change that.

There are four 'servant songs' in Isaiah's prophecies – four short poems that referred to someone who would come as both servant and liberator of Israel – which Jennens adapted for his libretto:

> He was despised and rejected of men, a man of sorrows and acquainted with grief.
>
> (From Isa. 53:3)

> He gave His back to the smiters, and His cheeks to them that plucked off His hair: He hid not His face from shame and spitting.
>
> (From Isa. 53:7)

> Surely He hath borne our griefs, and carried our
> sorrows! He was wounded for our transgressions, He
> was bruised for our iniquities; the chastisement of our
> peace was upon Him.
>
> (From Isa. 53:4–5)

The servant is variously interpreted as referring to Israel in exile, or to Cyrus the Great who, in liberating Israel, became God's servant. Later the servant songs were reappropriated to give meaning to the Maccabean martyrs – a rebel army of Jews in the second century BC who fought against the Hellenisation of Judaism and liberated Judea from the Seleucid empire. They suffered heavy casualties, but were regarded as heroes. The book of Maccabees echoes Isaiah's words:

> We are suffering these things on our own account,
> because of our sins against our own God.
>
> (2 Maccabees 7:18 NRSV)

Whereas Isaiah saw the suffering as borne by the whole nation, the Maccabean account shows innocent individuals taking on suffering on behalf of others. This transformation laid the groundwork for the idea of one man – Jesus – suffering on behalf of the whole community. Whatever Isaiah may have had in mind, it is easy to see why these words so readily became descriptive of Jesus, who was beaten and crucified, despite his innocence.

'I Know That My Redeemer Liveth' is one of the most famous arias from *Messiah*, and the delicacy and elegance of the soprano line perfectly suits its source – for, despite the confident-sounding lyrics, in its biblical context it is not a song of triumph like the 'Hallelujah Chorus', but a combination of Job's song of hope in devastated circumstances and St Paul's anticipation of life beyond death.

> I know that my Redeemer liveth, and that He shall stand at the latter day upon the earth; and though worms destroy this body, yet in my flesh shall I see God.
>
> (From Job 19:25–6)

> For now is Christ risen from the dead, the first-fruits of them that sleep.
>
> (From 1 Cor. 15:20)

In the middle of Job's suffering, his statement was a declaration of stubborn faith against the odds (and Handel's placing of the word 'stand' on a long, sustained note emphasises the point). But by adding St Paul's words to Job's, Jennens further invests Job's words with the idea that there would be a resurrection of all believers.

God as the Shepherd of his people is a recurring metaphor in the Old Testament. By tying this theme together with the nativity story, Jennens makes a theological comment – the shepherds visit the infant Jesus, but Jesus himself is both the Shepherd of his people and the Lamb of God who himself becomes a sacrifice for them.

> He shall feed His flock like a shepherd; and He shall gather the lambs with His arm, and carry them in His

bosom, and shall gently lead those that are with young.

(From Isa. 40:11)

All we like sheep have gone astray; we have turned every one to his own way; and the Lord hath laid on him the iniquity of us all.

(From Isa. 53:6)

Behold the Lamb of God, that taketh away the sins of the world.

(From John 1:29)

Most of the texts Jennens chose had long been recognised in Christian thought as anticipating Jesus as Messiah, and certainly the picture they summon up of a suffering servant, a shepherd, a saviour, redeemer and king fit well with Christian thought. But it is noticeable that Jennens's choices laid particularly heavy emphasis on the idea of Jesus as King, especially by including several royal psalms. It seems that into the spiritual message of *Messiah*, Jennens was weaving his own controversial views concerning the English monarchy. For Charles Jennens was a non-juror.

The non-juror schism began in 1688 when James II went into exile. James had converted to Catholicism early in his life, which initially did not prove to be an issue when he succeeded to the throne at the age of fifty-one. But during the three years of his reign he made several moves to give Catholics more freedom in public life and to foster religious tolerance. There was a widespread fear of Catholicism, however, and James was gradually alienating all his supporters. When his wife Mary, who was also a Roman Catholic, gave birth to a son (James Stuart, the father of Bonnie

Prince Charlie), it seemed that a Roman Catholic dynasty would be established. So when William of Orange invaded in 1688, the fact that he was a Protestant made it easy for him to gain a following. With very little resistance William and Mary were made joint monarchs and James fled to France, where he spent the rest of his life in exile until his death in 1701.

Anglican clergy, though, were required to swear an oath of loyalty to their monarch. While they were willing to accept William and Mary as regents, nine bishops and about four hundred Anglican clergy would not swear the oath of allegiance to them and remained loyal in principle to the Jacobites. As a result many of them suffered poverty and some degree of persecution, but they stayed true to their conviction that it was their duty to preserve the true Anglican succession. Some of the separatists abandoned the schism when James II died in 1701, but others continued faithful to the Jacobite dynasty. The schism weakened after the Second Jacobite Rebellion of 1745, when Charles Edward Stuart (Bonnie Prince Charlie) tried and failed to retake the throne. It then came to a natural end when Charles himself died in 1788, and almost all of the remaining non-jurors took the oath to George III.

Jennens had lived as a non-juror through many years of this schism, which was still a live issue when he was producing his libretto. And it seems that, either deliberately or subconsciously, this preoccupation led him to place a particularly strong emphasis on the importance of Jesus Christ as, above all, the true and rightful King:

And the Gentiles shall come to thy light, and kings to the brightness of thy rising.

> (From Isa. 60:2–3 KJV)

For unto us a child is born, unto us a son is given, and the government shall be upon His shoulder; and His name shall be called Wonderful, Counsellor, the Mighty God, the Everlasting Father, the Prince of Peace.

> (From Isa. 9:6)

Rejoice greatly, O daughter of Zion; shout, O daughter of Jerusalem! Behold, thy King cometh unto thee; He is the righteous Saviour, and He shall speak peace unto the heathen.

> (From Zech. 9:9–10)

Lift up your heads, O ye gates; and be ye lift up, ye everlasting doors; and the King of Glory shall come in. Who is this King of Glory? The Lord strong and mighty, The Lord mighty in battle ... The Lord of Hosts, He is the King of Glory.

> (From Ps. 24:7–10)

In particular, Jennens adopts scriptures that are specifically taken to be messianic prophecies, such as Psalm 2, which Handel set as a bass solo – arguing that people do not recognise the Messiah as King. There is a possible parallel here with the non-juring schism:

Why do the nations so furiously rage together, and why do the people imagine a vain thing? The kings of the earth rise up, and the rulers take counsel together against the Lord, and against His anointed. Let us break their bonds asunder, and cast away their yokes from us.

(From Ps. 2:1–3)

He that dwelleth in Heav'n shall laugh them to scorn; The Lord shall have them in derision.

(From Ps. 2:4)

Thou shalt break them with a rod of iron; thou shalt dash them in pieces like a potter's vessel.

(Ps. 2:9)

Similarly, the 'Hallelujah Chorus' takes images of monarchy from the book of Revelation:

For the Lord God Omnipotent reigneth.

(From Rev. 19:6)

The kingdom of this world is become the kingdom of our Lord, and of His Christ; and He shall reign for ever and ever.

(From Rev. 11:15)

Jennens may have had personal and political reasons for his choice of scriptures for the libretto, but his greater achievement was to gather together the grand Old Testament metaphors for God and his Messiah, weaving them around just a few sentences from the Gospels to create a work that was more theological meditation than historical narrative. The shepherds in Luke's Gospel come to see the baby Jesus, but Isaiah's words shift the focus to God as the great Shepherd of the human race. Three kings from the Orient come to worship Jesus, and the reply immediately comes that Jesus himself is the King of kings and Lord of lords. Wonderful, Counsellor, Mighty God, Everlasting Father, Prince of Peace, King, Messiah, Servant and Shepherd – Jennens's selections from the text were submitted to Handel's talent and his music gave them wings. For Handel's listeners, just as for Handel himself, whether *Messiah* is encountered from a religious perspective or purely as a musical feast, surely no one could fail to be moved by the grandeur of the words and music that call their listeners to look beyond the limits of their own horizon.

8
Gospel truth

The New Testament begins with four Gospels – the story of Jesus Christ as told by Matthew, Mark, Luke and John, who are known as the Evangelists. Not to be confused with 'evangelical' – a style of modern Christianity – an evangelist is simply someone who broadcasts good news. The four Gospels have a lot in common, but the details and the perspective vary from one account to the next. Matthew is especially concerned with the connections between Jesus and Jewish history and tradition, and highlights the continuity between them, although it is a matter of debate as to whether he places this in a positive or a negative light. Mark writes more briskly, with an as-it-happens news reporter style. Luke is a great storyteller, including a lot more characters and bringing each one to life, and giving particular attention to the undervalued – women, non-Jews and outcasts. John is a mystic and philosopher, who pays at least as much attention to underlying meanings as to factual accounts. The Gospels make up less than a tenth of the whole Bible, but because they record the life and teachings of Jesus, their significance for Western culture far outweighs their length. They provide the undercurrent, if not the main subject matter, to countless numbers of paintings, songs, oratorios, hymns, sculptures, poems, plays and novels of the last two thousand years.

The phrase 'gospel truth' is sometimes used to imply a quality of unvarnished, straightforward honesty – nothing but the facts. But just how true are the Gospels, with their strange stories of angels and miracles? If you compare them to other kinds of writing – biography, history, religious dogma – you discover first of all that the Gospels are not fiction. They tie in with the framework of other historical sources, which confirm that there really was a religious leader called Jesus Christ, that he had many followers, and that he died by crucifixion. So the Gospels are accounts of real people's lives. But they are not biographical in the modern sense of the word – they say very little about Jesus' personality or the details of his personal life, focusing instead on the interpretation of his acts and teachings. So the Gospels are not fiction or fantasy, but neither are they an unvarnished, unbiased record of events (although it would be true to say that very little history is written like that!). The specific purpose of the Gospels was not only to record Jesus' life, but also to interpret its significance and to pass on the teachings of the early church. The Gospels, then, are a kind of history-plus – true stories, carefully selected and arranged, and woven through with religious interpretation. A Gospel is a genre all of its own, and it is useful to remember this when reading something that, from a twenty-first-century perspective, seems to lurch between history and fantasy fiction.

Annunciation

Nowhere is the story of Jesus more loaded with strange events than his birth, which is surrounded by angels, astrological signs, prophecies and miracles. It begins with the annunciation, an angelic announcement of his birth:

> God sent the angel Gabriel to Nazareth, a town in Galilee, to a virgin pledged to be married to a man named Joseph, a descendant of David. The virgin's name was Mary. The angel went to her and said, 'Greetings, you who are highly favoured! The Lord is with you.'
>
> Mary was greatly troubled at his words and wondered what kind of greeting this might be. But the angel said to her, 'Do not be afraid, Mary, you have found favour with God. You will conceive and give birth to a son, and you are to call him Jesus. He will be great and will be called the Son of the Most High. The Lord God will give him the throne of his father David, and he will reign over the house of Jacob forever; his kingdom will never end.'
>
> 'How will this be,' Mary asked the angel, 'since I am a virgin?'
>
> The angel answered, 'The Holy Spirit will come on you, and the power of the Most High will overshadow you. So the holy one to be born will be called the Son of God. Even Elizabeth your relative is going to have a child in her old age, and she who was said to be

unable to conceive is in her sixth month. For no word from God will ever fail.'

'I am the Lord's servant,' Mary answered. 'May it be to me according to your word.' Then the angel left her.

(Luke 1:26–38)

The angel Gabriel is the chief of God's messengers in the Bible, so a message delivered by him was a really big deal. Angels feature regularly in the Bible, and sometimes they are described as fantastic, luminous, winged creatures, while at other times they appear in human form. But here Luke does not say what Gabriel looked like, which has left the interpretation open to artists and poets.

Medieval and classical annunciations were often packed with symbolism. The angel was nearly always shown on the left of the picture, because in both classical and biblical tradition a chief servant always stood at his master's right hand (that is the origin of the phrase 'right-hand man') – so the angel must be at the right hand of Mary and Jesus. Mary and the angel are usually separated by some architectural feature, such as a column, emphasising the fact that they live in different dimensions, and the angel often has something in his hand: in early frescoes and mosaics it is a messenger's staff, but it evolves over time into a sceptre (a symbol of God's power) or a branch of lilies. Even the flowers in these pictures have symbolic meaning: roses represent Mary herself, lilies symbolise her purity, and there is sometimes an open door leading into a walled rose garden, which indicates Mary's virginity.

Fra Angelico painted the annunciation several times,

following different variations on these themes. In his *Altarpiece of the Annunciation* (c. 1430–2, Museo del Prado, Madrid), he followed the Eastern tradition of seating Mary on a golden throne, with stars overhead symbolising the universe, and to the left he added Adam and Eve being evicted from the garden of Eden. This placed Mary in medieval tradition as the Queen of Heaven, and also as the 'new Eve'. The idea was that sin had come into the world through Adam and Eve, and had been handed down from one generation to the next. But Mary was protected from sin by God's grace (this is what the immaculate conception means), and subsequently Jesus was conceived without inheriting the taint of sin. He became 'the second Adam' – the beginning of a new era of humanity, and because of this, Mary was venerated because she had been the agent of the reversal of the fall.

A few years later Fra Angelico painted a much simpler version of the annunciation (1438–45, Museo di San Marco, Florence). This time he set the scene amid classical architecture, with Mary seated on a plain wooden stool, wearing the colours of royalty, but in other respects appearing quite human. The angel and Mary look directly at each other, indicating communication between heaven and earth, and they bow towards each other with crossed hands as a sign of mutual reverence but also in acknowledgement that they are in the presence of the holy.

The features of some annunciations come not from the Bible, but from the Gospel (or Protoevangelium) of James, written about AD 150, which says that Mary was spinning purple thread for the temple, went outside to fetch a jug of water, and there the angel spoke to her. This is why Mary is often shown seated at a spinning wheel, with a water jug nearby (sometimes the jug becomes a vase for the lilies). These features are abandoned in later Western paintings and instead Mary is shown either reading an open book of Scripture, emphasising the idea that Jesus comes in fulfilment of the Scriptures, or kneeling by a *prie-dieu* (a kneeler, sometimes with a little cupboard for a Bible or prayer books) which holds the Word of God in written form, mirroring the idea that the child in Mary's womb is 'the Word made flesh':

> And the Word became flesh and lived among us, and we have seen his glory.
>
> (John 1:14 NRSV)

Eastern images treat the annunciation (the announcement by the angel) and the incarnation (the actual moment of conception) as two separate events, but Western art often conflates them, adding to the annunciation some rays of light shining like a spotlight onto Mary, and a dove representing the Holy Spirit flying in this light or hovering above Mary, to indicate the miraculous conception of Jesus. Medieval images also complete the reference to the Trinity by including God the Father as a hand pointing or a face looking down from the sky. The one figure in the event who only appears rarely is Joseph (Mary's husband), though occasionally he is seen at work in the background.

There is a Latin prayer known as the *Angelus* (Latin for 'angel') that begins with Gabriel's first words to Mary and then intersperses her response, 'Let it be to me according to thy word', with three recitations of the *Ave Maria*. The origins of the *Angelus* prayer are uncertain, but for seven hundred years or more it has been recited three times a day in many convents and monasteries, and it has also been set to music, one recent and very beautiful example being Franz Biebl's *Ave Maria* (1964).

A painting called *The Angelus* hangs in the Musée D'Orsay in Paris, painted by Jean-François Millet (1814–75), who was one of Van Gogh's heroes. It is a work with an interesting history, an evening scene with two figures standing in a field, bowing slightly and with hands crossed, with a basket at their feet. Commissioned by Thomas G. Appleton of Boston, Massachusetts, its original title was *Prayer for the Potato Crop*. But Mr Appleton never collected his painting, so Millet approached a friend to help him sell it, and the friend suggested he might alter the painting and change its title. Millet repainted the basket, added a church steeple in the background, and named it *The Angelus*. The man and the woman face each other, the woman bowing slightly with her hands crossed, alluding to the traditional annunciations. But with no rays of light, no angel's wings and none of the traditional symbolism, the renamed painting opens up new layers of interpretation, with a genuinely poor and rural woman and an angel who – as in the story of Jacob wrestling – appears in human form. Whether Millet's renaming of his picture ended up producing a thoroughly human depiction of the annunciation, or whether the new title served to dignify ordinary human love, is left to the viewer to decide. But revisiting the annunciation in a simplified manner is something that twentieth-century artists and poets have also done to great effect.

Polish sculptor Igor Mitoraj (b. 1944) makes figures of classical proportions, but in a postmodern twist on the broken limbs of once-perfect classical statues, he deliberately truncates them so that from the start his figures are fragmentary – disembodied heads, or torsos without limbs. Mitoraj's *Doors of the Annunciation* at the Basilica of St Mary's of the Angels and Martyrs in Rome (2006) sweep away most of the traditional symbolism of the annunciation, and what remains is simply a monumental figure of a winged angel emerging from the bronze high up on the left door, while Mary bows below him on the right door. The two figures are subtly separated by the crack between the doors, but connected by a smooth path in the otherwise textured bronze. If one stands directly in front of the doors and looks at the two figures, their unadorned simplicity makes them all the more impressive – but while the angel is a winged creature of classical proportions, the deliberate incompleteness that Mitoraj gives his figures affects the perception of them. When we encounter classical statues – whether marble or bronze – with an arm or a head missing, we make a mental adjustment, knowing that although they have survived incomplete, they were created as perfect, human form idealised. Mitoraj, though, gives us human figures that are both exaggerated into classical proportions and deliberately incomplete, which conveys an awareness that for all our aspirations and ideals, human existence is always fragmented and never perfectible.

One of the features of the sculpture is that, even though the figures emerge from a flat background, what you see in the work still depends upon where you stand. Looking directly at the doors from the square, you see the elegant simplicity of his restatement of the traditional theme. But move a little closer and you see another feature that recurs in Mitoraj's work: a hidden face within one of the figures. In this case, a rectangle is cut in the angel's wing and there is another face peering through. There are different ways this could be interpreted – for instance, it plays straight back into Mitoraj's habit of fragmenting and displacing body parts. From a theological point of view, you could see the face in the wing as the face of Christ, whose birth the angel is announcing, or of the Holy Spirit, whom the angel promises will be the agent of incarnation. But the image is equally suggestive of the idea that a message from God is never an indirect or disconnected communication. Marshall McLuhan coined the phrase 'the medium is the message' to emphasise that the way a message is delivered becomes an integral part of its meaning. But his adage is not a bad approximation of the theological idea that God's message is God himself, made real through the birth of Christ. Another important idea that Mitoraj projects, however, is that the face in the angel's wing is most clearly visible from Mary's viewpoint, standing just below her figure and looking up, which is strongly suggestive of the idea that, despite the extremely lowly position of women at that time, Mary was not merely a pawn in the game, but a significant player in the story. Here her point of view is given its proper dignity, rather than sublimating her experience to the interpretation of theological onlookers.

Allowing Mary to be viewed as a real woman, and not a symbolic icon, is further achieved by several poets writing in the twentieth century, including U.A. Fanthorpe, Luci Shaw, Edwin Muir and Noel Rowe, all of whom have elegantly and imaginatively retold events from Mary's point of view. Luke's account (see above) reads almost as if the conversation between Mary and the angel took place in two minutes flat, with an inevitability about Mary's response, as if she had no choice but to say 'yes' to God. But Edwin Muir (1887–1959), in his poem 'Annunciation', created a scene where, while the ordinary things of life continue with their random sounds, the meeting between Mary and the angel might have been a lengthy encounter – and a whole afternoon passed while they gazed into each other's faces. Muir captured perfectly the theological idea that while a message from God may be impressive, it is never impersonal. It is not just a delivery of information, like an email from head office, but a meeting of persons, and the primary significance of the angel's visitation is not the angel himself, nor even the message that he bears, but the connection made between a person and God. (And, as some theologians have mused, perhaps Mary also needed time because she had a choice to make – she had the option to say 'no'.)

While Muir hinted delicately at a length and intensity of encounter uncharacteristic of traditional interpretations, Australian poet Noel Rowe, in 'Magnificat',[1] made the encounter timeless – one of those experiences where you are so absorbed in what is happening that you lose your sense of time passing, and a moment can seem like an hour. He also wove in a thread of eroticism, pointing out later in an essay[2] that his purpose was not to be deliberately sensational, but to suggest that the closest we might get to describing the depth of connection between human and divine is by analogy with the intimacy of lovers.

> The angel did not draw attention to himself.
> He came in. So quietly I could hear
> my blood beating on the shore of absolute
> beauty. There was fear, yes, but also
> faith among familiar things:

light, just letting go the wooden chair,
my knife cutting through the hard skin
of vegetable, hitting wood, and the noise
outside of children playing with their dog,
throwing him a bone. Then all these sounds
dropped out of hearing. The breeze
drew back, let silence come in first,
and my heart, my heart, was wanting him,
reaching out, and taking hold of smooth-muscled
    fire.
And it was done. I heard the children laugh
and saw the dog catch the scarred bone.

Rowe's angel seems to slip subtly into the clatter of everyday events, but with a presence that is met with urgent longing from Mary. These poetic meditations draw out the fact that Christian thought embraces both the transcendent 'otherness' of God, and the idea that through Jesus Christ and the Holy Spirit, God penetrates deep within the life of a believer. Both poets capture something of the belief that Jesus Christ reconciles the paradoxical mixture of divine and human, so that God can be encountered as both transcendent and intimately close.

Nativity

The tradition of a midwinter festival in England long predates Jesus, but once Christianity became the common religion of Europe, the midwinter festival was adapted to become the celebration of the birth of Jesus – hence the name

'Christmas', which is a conflation of 'Christ's Mass'. The stories of Jesus' birth come from Matthew's and Luke's Gospels. Luke seems to have had more inside information on Jesus' family – in fact some scholars believe that Luke knew Mary, or some other close relatives of Jesus, because various details only known to the family, including the events of the night of Jesus' birth, are unique to his Gospel.

> In those days Caesar Augustus issued a decree that a census should be taken of the entire Roman world. (This was the first census that took place while Quirinius was governor of Syria.) And everyone went to their own town to register.
>
> So Joseph also went up from the town of Nazareth in Galilee to Judea, to Bethlehem the town of David, because he belonged to the house and line of David. He went there to register with Mary, who was pledged to be married to him and was expecting a child. While they were there, the time came for the baby to be born, and she gave birth to her firstborn, a son. She wrapped him in cloths and placed him in a manger, because there was no guest room available for them.
>
> And there were shepherds living out in the fields nearby, keeping watch over their flocks at night. An angel of the Lord appeared to them, and the glory of the Lord shone around them, and they were terrified. But the angel said to them, 'Do not be afraid. I bring you good news of great joy that will be for all the people. Today in the town of David a Saviour has been born to you; he is the Messiah, the Lord. This will be

a sign to you: You will find a baby wrapped in cloths and lying in a manger.'

Suddenly a great company of the heavenly host appeared with the angel, praising God and saying,

'Glory to God in the highest heaven,
and on earth peace to those on whom his favour
    rests.'

When the angels had left them and gone into heaven, the shepherds said to one another, 'Let's go to Bethlehem and see this thing that has happened, which the Lord has told us about.'

So they hurried off and found Mary and Joseph, and the baby, who was lying in the manger. When they had seen him, they spread the word concerning what had been told them about this child, and all who heard it were amazed at what the shepherds said to them. But Mary treasured up all these things and pondered them in her heart. The shepherds returned, glorifying and praising God for all the things they had heard and seen, which were just as they had been told.

(Luke 2:1–20)

Luke notes that Jesus was laid in a manger – an animal's feeding trough. The remains of most of the first-century houses discovered around Jerusalem and Bethlehem show that animal pens were usually within the house itself, either as a central room within the house, or as a lower floor dug out beneath the main room. The place traditionally kept as Jesus' birthplace in Bethlehem, unlike the chilly looking stable scenes of Western art, is a dug-out cave below the ground with a steady year-round temperature of around 67°F (20°C). But artists have always interpreted biblical and classical stories according to their own cultural settings, and so it is that the traditional European setting for the nativity was a large garden shed.

The adoration of the Magi

There's a glorious clash of cultures in nativity scenes – Mary the peasant girl is often seated among animals and shepherds dressed in royal robes to indicate that she is the Queen of Heaven. And it is even more exaggerated in scenes called *The Adoration of the Magi*, where in the midst of the rural stable setting, three men dressed in royal robes kneel in the dust, bowing before the Madonna and child and presenting lavish gifts. Some of these features are layers of tradition that have been added over time, but the bare bones of the story come from Matthew's Gospel:

> After Jesus was born in Bethlehem in Judea, during the time of King Herod, Magi from the east came to Jerusalem and asked, 'Where is the one who has been born king of the Jews? We saw his star when it rose and have come to worship him.'
>
> When King Herod heard this he was disturbed, and all Jerusalem with him. When he had called together all the people's chief priests and teachers of the law, he asked them where the Messiah was to be born. 'In

Bethlehem in Judea,' they replied, 'for this is what the prophet has written:

> '"But you, Bethlehem, in the land of Judah,
> are by no means least among the rulers of Judah;
> for out of you will come a ruler
> who will shepherd my people Israel."'

Then Herod called the Magi secretly and found out from them the exact time the star had appeared. He sent them to Bethlehem and said, 'Go and make a careful search for the child. As soon as you find him, report to me, so that I too may go and worship him.'

After they had heard the king, they went on their way, and the star they had seen when it rose went ahead of them until it stopped over the place where the child was. When they saw the star they were overjoyed. On coming to the house, they saw the child with his mother Mary, and they bowed down and worshipped him. Then they opened their treasures and presented him with gifts of gold, frankincense and myrrh. And having been warned in a dream not to go back to Herod, they returned to their country by another route.

(Matt. 2:1–12)

These visitors, whom Milton refers to as 'star-led wizards',[3] are variously referred to as Magi, wise men, or kings. 'Wise men' is a translation of Matthew's original Greek word *magoi* (*magi* in Latin). A preference for the term 'wise men' developed in English, because the word *magi* seemed too closely associated with magic. But in the original context – at a time when astrology was synonymous with astronomy and was considered a serious science – a magus referred to someone who studied the stars and interpreted dreams. The Magi are commonly thought to have been Persian, the priest-scholars of Zoroastrianism.

Over time, Christian tradition gradually transformed the Magi into three kings. The early Christian writer Tertullian (born c. AD 160) made the link between the Magi and some Old Testament prophecies about foreign visitors bringing gifts to the Messiah:

> Nations shall come to your light,
> and kings to the brightness of your dawn . . .
> They shall bring gold and frankincense,
> and shall proclaim the praise of the Lord.
>> (Isa. 60:3–6 NRSV)

> The kings of Tarshish and of distant shores
> will bring tribute to him;
> the kings of Sheba and Seba
> will present him gifts.
>> (Ps. 72:10 NIV)

> Because of your temple at Jerusalem,
> kings will bring you gifts.
>> (Ps. 68:29 NIV)

While Tertullian called them 'Magi-Kings', one of his contemporaries, Origen, imagined that there were three of them since they brought three gifts. Irenaeus of Lyons had pointed out that the three gifts were symbolic of Christ's three roles, and this was also woven into the tradition: gold for a king, frankincense for a deity, and myrrh for his mortality and to foretell his untimely death.

Byzantine art shows the Magi as indistinguishable from each other, dressed in identical Persian or Arabic tunics and trousers, with soft hats or Phrygian caps. But by the tenth century, they were more commonly depicted as kings with crowns, and were given distinct identities – one Caucasian, one Asian and one African, representing the three continents of the Old World which were taken to be the descendants of the three sons of Noah. From as early as the sixth century they were given various names in different languages, but their Latin names – Caspar, Melchior and Balthasar – were the ones that became established, and these appear in *The Golden Legend*, a life of the saints written by Jacobus de Voragine in about 1260. In the Germanic tradition Caspar is always shown as an elderly Caucasian man carrying the gold, while Melchior, a middle-aged Asian, brings the frankincense, and Balthasar is a young African and carries the myrrh.

In the twelfth century, relics said to belong to the three kings were taken to Cologne, Germany, where a legend grew up that the three Magi were reunited in AD 54 to celebrate Christmas and where shortly afterwards all three of them died. Traditions surrounding the Magi remain strong in that part of Germany where, on the sixth of January, 'star singers' go from house to house singing Epiphany carols and sprinkling the doorways with water. The initials C+B+M are chalked over the doorposts, which originally stood for Caspar, Melchior and Balthasar, but later took on another meaning: *Christus Mansionem Benedictat* ('Christ bless this home').

The story of the Magi is laced more subtly through later work. T.S. Eliot's 'The Journey of the Magi' focuses only indirectly on the nativity scene, making more of the journey as a symbol of life and drawing connections between birth and death. The Magi also lurk in the shadows at the opening of Salley Vickers's novel, *Miss Garnet's Angel*. The feast of the Epiphany is the date when Vickers's unlikely heroine decides to set out on her journey to Venice, and the Magi then become woven into the narrative, not only because it begins with a gift and a long journey, but because the book of Tobit, which is the central motif, artfully links art, Judaism and Christianity with Zoroastrianism (Zoroaster being the first prophet of monotheism). Sally Vickers herself said that although some of those connections were deliberate, the Magi became a connecting motif by a happy accident, as she had decided upon the feast of the Epiphany as Miss Garnet's moment of inspiration for her journey before realising that the Magi were also connected with Zoroastrianism. There is something delightful about this seeming accident, given Matthew's account of the Magi's disrupted journey, which U.A. Fanthorpe described in her poem 'BC:AD' as 'haphazard':

> This was the moment when even energetic Romans
> Could find nothing better to do
> Than counting heads in remote provinces.
> And this was the moment
> When a few farm workers and three
> Members of an obscure Persian sect

Walked haphazard by starlight straight
Into the kingdom of heaven.[4]

Seen retrospectively, the birth of Christ became the moment by which time has been divided ever since; a moment which, like a wrinkle in time, created a doorway into another dimension and changed the course of history. But Fanthorpe captures eloquently the fact that when it actually happened, no one really knew or understood the huge impact Jesus was going to have, or how his life would unfold. The nativity scenes we see in galleries are layered over with religious symbolism, but they are events that, when they actually occurred, probably seemed relatively unremarkable, or at most happy accidents.

In the beginning (reprise)

The fourth Gospel does not record any stories about the birth of Jesus, but instead gives a mystical, theological account of the coming of Jesus, which also owes something to Greek philosophy. As noted in chapter 1, John borrowed the opening words of Genesis for the opening of his Gospel, and then introduced a contrast between light and darkness, which is a theme he focuses on all the way through his Gospel:

> In him was life, and that life was the light of all people. The light shines in the darkness, and the darkness has not overcome it.
>
> (John 1:4–5)

This is an echo of Isaiah's words, 'The people walking in darkness have seen a great light . . .' (Isa. 9:2).

The darkness and light motif is one of the threads that run through the discussion of ghosts in *Hamlet*. Elizabethan anxiety over the clash of Catholic and Protestant ideas forms the undercurrent to several of Shakespeare's plays, and in *Hamlet* confusion reigns as to whether a ghost should be regarded as good or malign – an appearance of a departed spirit returning from beyond the grave with an important message, or an illusion that came from hell itself. Marcellus considers the Protestant idea that Christ's birth so effectively banished the darkness, that every time Christmas was celebrated even the night was as light as day:

> Some say that ever 'gainst that season comes
> Wherein our Saviour's birth is celebrated,
> This bird of dawning singeth all night long;
> And then, they say, no spirit dare stir abroad,
> The nights are wholesome, then no planets strike,
> No fairy takes, nor witch hath power to charm,
> So hallowed and so gracious is that time.[5]

The Protestant idea prevails here, that spirits and ghosts were part of the darkness, and the light of Christ, by contrast, banished the darkness and pervaded the night with goodness, health and light. The pairing of the words 'hallowed' and 'gracious' again picks up the paradox of a God who is holy and transcendent, yet also accessible in his self-giving. Grace, by definition, is a freely given, undeserved goodness.

Nunc Dimittis (A Love Supreme)

John Coltrane, one of the most famous and admired jazz saxophonists of the age, was at the height of his powers in 1965, when *A Love Supreme* won him two Grammys and enormous critical acclaim and became his biggest-selling album. But life had not always flowed so smoothly for 'the Trane'. Through the 1950s he had nearly been destroyed by drug addiction, until a religious encounter gave him the strength to kick the habit. *A Love Supreme* was Coltrane's expression of gratitude to God, and ranges from the jubilation of a song of praise to a wistful, searching quality that suggests an ongoing spiritual quest.

No two performances of any piece of music are ever identical. They are affected not only by the musicians themselves, but by the rehearsal, the size and atmosphere of the venue and the mood of the audience. But just occasionally there are nights when not only do all the components come together perfectly, but it seems some intangible element lifts an already great performance into another dimension. There was just such a night for *A Love Supreme*. As 'the Trane' and his band performed, every last ounce of their skill and musicianship met in an absolutely magical performance, and it seemed almost as if he had touched heaven. As he walked offstage, his drummer heard him breathe just two words: '*Nunc Dimittis.*'

Music lovers will recognise those two words as the title of many a piece of sacred music. Geoffrey Burgon's *Nunc Dimittis* was popularised as the theme tune for the TV series *Tinker, Tailor, Soldier, Spy* in 1979. A *Nunc Dimittis* may feature in concerts by composers as various as Haydn and Arvo Pärt, and every day of the year, in any cathedral in the land, half-way through the evening service the choir will sing a *Nunc Dimittis*. But why, at that moment when he felt he had given the performance of his lifetime, were these the words on John Coltrane's lips?

The *Nunc Dimittis* originated as a four-line song that comes from the nativity story. A few days after he was born, Mary and Joseph took Jesus to the temple to be dedicated to God, and there in the temple was an elderly prophet named Simeon. He was convinced that he would not die until he had seen the coming of the Messiah. By some sixth sense, when he saw the baby, he believed that this was the Messiah he was waiting for, and these are the words he said:

> Lord, now let your servant depart in peace,
>   according to your word.
> For my eyes have seen your salvation
> Which you have prepared in the sight of all people
> A light for revelation to the Gentiles, and for glory
>   to your people Israel.
>
> (From Luke 2:29–32)

Nunc Dimittis: 'now dismiss'. It is a prayer of completion. Now you can let me go. Now I can die a happy man, because my life is fulfilled and I have done what I came for.

The *Nunc Dimittis* is often said at funerals and at evening prayers, because, as has been known intuitively for gener-ations and explained by modern psychology, every time we go to sleep it is like a mini-death. But the *Nunc Dimittis* also crops up in literature time and again as a signal of an ending and a new beginning.

The *Nunc Dimittis* is sometimes used – either in full, or just as two words – simply to mean 'it's all over'. In *The Once and Future King*, T.H. White's brilliant retelling of the Arthurian legend, once Arthur has made his declaration of chivalry and sworn an oath that he will only ever use his powers for good, Merlyn realises that his role as Arthur's mentor and teacher is over, and he expresses this succinctly and elegantly by reciting the *Nunc Dimittis*.[6]

In 1921 the first performance was given of a science-fiction play, *R.U.R.* (Rossum's Universal Robots), by Czech play-wright Karel Čapek. The play is set in a factory that makes robots closely resembling human beings. Eventually the robots gain language, in an episode reminiscent of the Tower of Babel, and eventually all the humans are exterminated by the robots except for one, named Alquist. He quotes the *Nunc Dimittis* as an indication that in its own endeavour to control the world, the human race has inadvertently anni-hilated itself.

Roald Dahl used the phrase similarly in one of his short stories, although with a sinister twist. The narrator, Lionel Lampson, recounts how a few days earlier he played a cruel trick on his girlfriend Janet, humiliating her in public. But he smugly boasts that he got away with it because he has now received a note from her saying that he is forgiven, and a peace offering – a jar of caviar, his favourite food. In fact, he says, he may have eaten a little too much of it, as he is suddenly feeling rather ill. And there the story ends. But Dahl put his usual twist in the tale simply through his choice of title: *Nunc Dimittis*.

Such twists and turns in meaning can invest *Nunc Dimittis* with sadness, resignation, cynicism, horror or humour. But of all these, it was John Coltrane's utterance that had most in common with Simeon's words. Now, Lord, I can die happy. My life is fulfilled; I have done what I came for.

John the Baptist

In the National Gallery hangs a particularly gruesome picture by Caravaggio, in which a beautiful young woman carries a large serving plate, her head turned away. Her face suggests distaste, or perhaps sorrow, while on the plate, instead of food, is the freshly cut-off head of a man.

The unfortunate man who lost his head was John the Baptist, the cousin of Jesus. John appears in the Gospels at the beginning of Jesus' adult life and, as his name suggests, he spent his time baptising people – a ritual practice where people would be completely immersed in water as a sign of purification. John was renowned as a holy man, and there were some who thought he was the Messiah, and a reincarnation of Elijah. But he declared himself simply as the herald of the true Messiah. As represented in the delicately beautiful *Baptism of Christ* by Piero della Francesca (also in the National Gallery), when John baptised Jesus the Holy Spirit appeared in the form of a dove, confirming Jesus as the Son of God. Not long after this Jesus embarked on his own ministry and John lost his life at the hands of Herod:

At that time Herod the ruler heard reports about Jesus; and he said to his servants, 'This is John the

Baptist; he has been raised from the dead, and for this reason these powers are at work in him.' For Herod had arrested John, bound him, and put him in prison on account of Herodias, his brother Philip's wife, because John had been telling him, 'It is not lawful for you to have her.' Though Herod wanted to put him to death, he feared the crowd, because they regarded him as a prophet. But when Herod's birthday came, the daughter of Herodias danced before the company, and she pleased Herod so much that he promised on oath to grant her whatever she might ask. Prompted by her mother, she said, 'Give me the head of John the Baptist here on a platter.' The king was grieved, yet out of regard for his oaths and for the guests, he commanded it to be given; he sent and had John beheaded in the prison. The head was brought on a platter and given to the girl, who brought it to her mother. His disciples came and took the body and buried it; then they went and told Jesus.

(Matt. 14:1–12 NRSV)

An elaboration of the Gospel accounts developed into the legendary *Dance of the Seven Veils*, which is also associated with the legend of Ishtar, the Babylonian goddess of fertility, who danced a striptease dance through seven gates into the underworld. One of Gustave Flaubert's *Three Tales* (1877) was called 'Herodias', in which the responsibility for John's death is placed squarely on the shoulders of Salomé's mother, while Salomé herself is shown as a malleable young girl who forgets John's name even as she asks for his beheading. But Oscar Wilde's 1891 play, *Salomé*, presents the heroine as far from innocent, and suggests that she has a bizarre sexual interest in John the Baptist. Richard Strauss's 1906 opera was based on Wilde's play, and the central feature is the 'Dance of the Seven Veils'. In 1906, Maud Allen's even more seductive production, *Vision of Salomé*, gained her considerable notoriety as 'The Salomé Dancer'. More recently Kim Wilde, Nick Cave, Sinead O'Connor and U2 are among artists who have used Salomé as an image of alluring but ultimately inaccessible sexuality.

Sermon on the Mount

Just as the events of Jesus' life have become a central feature of Western art, music and literature, so his teachings have worked their way all through our language and culture. His stories, conversations and pithy sayings have become highly quotable – not only for their strictly religious content, but because they encapsulate radically humanitarian views.

'The salt of the earth'; 'going the second mile'; 'let your yes be yes and your no be no'; 'an eye for an eye and a tooth for a tooth'; 'turn the other cheek'; 'pearls before swine'; 'the Lord's Prayer' ('Our Father who art in heaven . . .'); 'wolves in sheep's clothing'; 'you cannot serve God and mammon' – all these phrases are from the Sermon on the Mount (Matt. 5 – 7), which is a condensed summary of Jesus' main teachings. Matthew presents it as one long speech, but he probably collected lots of Jesus' sayings together and tidied them up for literary presentation. As well as being a treasure chest of common English phrases, it is the source of inspiration for a number of literary gems, such as *Measure for Measure*, in which

Shakespeare not only teases out the niceties of forgiveness and judgement, but also considers the relationship between action and intent: to what extent is good intent an excuse for a bad act, or vice versa? The King James (Authorised) Version of the Bible was not published until 1611, five years before Shakespeare's death (and, despite a number of urban myths, there is no evidence either that he was involved in translating it, or that parts of it are coded in homage to him). Shakespeare was familiar with earlier versions of the Bible in English – probably the Geneva Bible or the Bishops Bible[7] – so what he read would be something like this:

> Iudge not, that ye be not iudged. For with what iudgement ye iudge, ye shalbe iudged: And with what measure ye meate, it shalbe measured to you agayne.
>
> (Matt. 7:1–2, Bishops Bible, 1568)

> Do not judge, or you too will be judged. For in the same way you judge others, you will be judged, and with the measure you use, it will be measured to you.
>
> (TNIV)

The Sermon on the Mount is also woven into the background of *The Merchant of Venice*. Explorations of the play's religious themes usually focus on whether Shakespeare was promoting a pro- or anti-Semitic point of view (though it is probably truer to say that Shakespeare presents the issues and then leaves it to the audience to decide). But another important thread revolves around justice and retribution, which assumed knowledge of Jesus' reinterpretation of the old adage 'an eye for an eye', his replacement of retribution with grace, and his command to love your enemies:

> You have heard that it was said, 'An eye for an eye and
> a tooth for a tooth.' But I say to you, Do not resist an
> evildoer. But if anyone strikes you on the right cheek,
> turn the other also . . .
>
> You have heard that it was said, 'You shall love your
> neighbour and hate your enemy.' But I say to you,
> Love your enemies and pray for those who persecute
> you.
>
> (Matt. 5:38–9, 43–4 NRSV)

The Sermon on the Mount was famously lampooned with
hilarious irreverence by Monty Python. The famous scene
where those at the very back of the crowd mishear Jesus
as saying, 'Blessed are the cheesemakers,' before a fight
breaks out, is based on the first twelve verses of the sermon,
called 'The Beatitudes' because each one begins with
'Blessed . . .'.

> Blessed are the pure in heart, for they will see God.
> Blessed are the peacemakers, for they will be called
> children of God.
>
> (Matt. 5:7–9 NRSV)

Parables

Woven through Jesus' teaching were thirty parables – stories
drawn from life that seem to have a moral or a message. It
is a typical schoolroom RE answer that Jesus told parables
to make his point clear, but the truth is that they often had
a twist in the tale or an opaque quality that made them

puzzling and difficult to understand. Certainly Jesus' audience did not understand what he meant, and Jesus himself claimed that he used parables to make his point obscure. Once when Jesus' disciples asked why he did not make his meaning plain and clear, Jesus replied with a quote from an ancient prophecy: 'The knowledge of the secrets of the kingdom of God has been given to you, but to others I speak in parables, so that, "though seeing, they may not see; though hearing, they may not understand"' (Luke 8:10). Some scholars have suggested that he did this to make people think harder when his teaching was controversial, or perhaps that he used stories to sort out which members of his following were committed to his ideas and which simply liked to be entertained.

Perhaps it is because the parables are intriguing, and leave plenty of room for interpretation that they have survived through the centuries. But certainly they have proved a rich source for literature and art, and their interpretation has shifted over time. Of the thirty parables Jesus told, four in particular appeared frequently in medieval art – the wise and foolish virgins, Dives and Lazarus, the good Samaritan, and the prodigal son. Later, the sower became a recurrent feature in the work of Van Gogh.

It is thought that the parable of the wise and foolish virgins might have originated in the early church, long after Jesus' death. The first generation of Christians expected that Jesus Christ would literally return from heaven within their lifetime and take his followers with him to heaven, and this parable, which appears in Matthew 25:1–13, is a warning to be ready at all times. Dives and Lazarus, from Luke 16:27–31, was another parable of reward and punishment. As well as featuring in medieval paintings, it was adapted as an old English folk song which originally had its own tune. Later it was sung to a twentieth-century Irish melody, 'Star of County Down',[8] and this was the tune that Ralph Vaughan Williams used as the basis for his *Five Variants of Dives and Lazarus* (1939), and reworked again as 'Kingsfold', the tune for the popular hymn 'I Heard the voice of Jesus Say'.

The good Samaritan

The good Samaritan is one of Jesus' parables that has survived as a cultural icon into the modern era. Jesus' radical humanitarian teaching is that you should treat all people – even the ones you do not know or like, and regardless of political or religious divisions – with the same respect and care you would expect yourself. The preface to the story shows a religious lawyer trying to wriggle out of the uncomfortable implications of this by suggesting that surely there must be limits to compassion. The tenor of the lawyer's question is a bit like a child trying to bargain his way out of having to do the chores. The good Samaritan, a tale of pure, altruistic, humanitarian aid, is Jesus' nuanced answer to the question.

> On one occasion an expert in the law stood up to test Jesus. 'Teacher,' he asked, 'what must I do to inherit eternal life?'
>
> 'What is written in the Law?' he replied. 'How do you read it?'
>
> He answered, '"Love the Lord your God with all

your heart and with all your soul and with all your strength and with all your mind"; and, "Love your neighbour as yourself."'

'You have answered correctly,' Jesus replied. 'Do this and you will live.'

But he wanted to justify himself, so he asked Jesus, 'And who is my neighbour?'

In reply Jesus said: 'A man was going down from Jerusalem to Jericho, when he fell into the hands of robbers. They stripped him of his clothes, beat him and went away, leaving him half dead. A priest happened to be going down the same road, and when he saw the man, he passed by on the other side. So too, a Levite, when he came to the place and saw him, passed by on the other side. But a Samaritan, as he travelled, came where the man was; and when he saw him, he took pity on him. He went to him and bandaged his wounds, pouring on oil and wine. Then he put the man on his own donkey, brought him to an inn and took care of him. The next day he took out two denarii and gave them to the innkeeper. "Look after him," he said, "and when I return, I will reimburse you for any extra expense you may have."

'Which of these three do you think was a neighbour to the man who fell into the hands of robbers?'

The expert in the law replied, "The one who had mercy on him.'

Jesus told him, 'Go and do likewise.'

(Luke 10:25–37)

The road from Jerusalem to Jericho was one of the most dangerous roads in the region, surrounded on either side by sandy hillsides where bandits hid. Robbed and beaten, the unfortunate traveller lay defenceless and dying, his only hope being that another traveller might stop and help him. But what person would take the risk of stopping to help, knowing that they too would be likely to end up dead?

The background to the good Samaritan is that there were deep social divisions between first-century Jews and Samaritans. The priest and the Levite, men of the highest religious standing in Jewish society, would have been obligated to help the dying man if they had believed he was Jewish. But the man lay there stripped of his clothes and therefore unidentifiable, so they were able (conveniently) to assume he was a Samaritan, turn a blind eye and leave him to his fate. But the Samaritan, ignoring any question of obligation, helped the dying man at considerable expense as well as personal risk, just because he was a fellow human being. A story about a Samaritan hero cannot have made comfortable listening for the Jewish lawyer who asked the question.

As it stands, the parable works purely as a tale of compassion and humanitarian aid. But early Christianity invested it with further layers of meaning. Clement of Alexandria and Irenaeus, both writing in the second century AD, saw the good Samaritan as a symbol of Jesus, saving the fallen victim from the wounds of sin. Later, Origen, who was a pupil of Clement, wrote down the allegory. The man who was robbed represented Adam, and his wounds were sin. Jerusalem was paradise and Jericho the world. The robbers represented the powers of evil, the priest stood for the Law, and the Levite for the prophets. The Samaritan represented Jesus. The inn, as a place of welcome, symbolised the Church, and the Samaritan's promise to return represented the second coming of Christ.[9]

This allegorical interpretation was widespread through early Christianity, and appears in a number of medieval stained-glass windows in French cathedrals, including Bourges, Sens and a beautiful example at Chartres. It is a tradition in stained glass to depict two stories in parallel, one as an interpretation of the other. The upper part of the window at Chartres shows Adam and Eve leaving the garden of Eden, wounded by sin, and the lower part shows the parable of the good Samaritan as the reversal of their plight.

Similar layers of symbolism also appear in the fourteenth-century poem *Piers Plowman*:

> Where the Samaritan is seen as symbolic of Christ, riding like a heroic knight to rescue people from hell, and the washing of the man's wounds as a baptism in Christ's passion.[10]

The good Samaritan has been painted by countless artists. Rembrandt painted the roadside scene, and captured the helplessness and dead weight of the beaten man and the compassion of the Samaritan. *The Good Samaritan* by Delacroix (1849) gives an even more naturalistic depiction of the Samaritan's sturdy strength and the mixture of pain and relief on the face of the rescued man as he is manoeuvred onto the horse, while in the shadows a priest is departing past the empty and abandoned goods chest. One of the things that Van Gogh found soothing during periods of illness and mental distress was to produce paintings based on images by other artists. *The Good Samaritan (After Delacroix)* (May 1890) inverts the scene and delivers it in lighter, brighter colours, with plenty of his favourite yellow, the lighter colours making the departing figures of both the priest and the Levite more visible.

Among contemporary depictions, Chinese artist He Qi has painted *The Good Samaritan* using his trademark mixture of Chinese folk art and modern art techniques in brilliant colours to produce something more like a modern icon of the dying man and the Samaritan. But James B. Janknegt, in *Portrait of You as the Good Samaritan*, leaves the two main figures out of the picture altogether. The scene is transferred into a contemporary setting and painted with an upward perspective, as if you are looking up from the pavement, at a series of people hurrying along a road. The viewer gets the impression of what it would be like to be the suffering person on the roadside, deliberately excluded from the line of sight of those who pass by and will not help.

The prodigal son

The prodigal son is the most enduring and famous of all Jesus' parables and, like the good Samaritan, it is a story of disaster and restoration. But this time the person rescued is not a victim of violent crime, but a dissolute young man who brought all his troubles upon himself. Having left home with a share of the family fortune, he wasted it in riotous living, until he eventually returned home, hoping to get a menial job on his father's estate. There, unexpectedly, he was received with open arms and forgiven.

The story of the prodigal son (which is where the English phrase 'kill the fatted calf' comes from) has been painted dozens of times, and many of them show the son arriving at the father's house, on his knees or in his father's arms. If you reconstructed the parable from the paintings alone, you might get the impression that it was the depth of the son's regret that softened the father's heart. But it was a little more complicated than that.

> There was a man who had two sons. The younger one said to his father, 'Father, give me my share of the estate.' So he divided his property between them.
>
> Not long after that, the younger son got together all he had, set off for a distant country and there squandered his wealth in wild living. After he had spent everything, there was a severe famine in that whole country, and he began to be in need. So he went and hired himself out to a citizen of that country, who sent him to his fields to feed pigs. He longed to fill his stomach with the pods that the pigs were eating, but no-one gave him anything.
>
> When he came to his senses, he said, 'How many of my father's hired servants have food to spare, and here I am starving to death! I will set out and go back to my father and say to him: Father, I have sinned against heaven and against you. I am no longer worthy to be called your son; make me like one of your hired servants.' So he got up and went to his father.

But while he was still a long way off, his father saw him and was filled with compassion for him; he ran to his son, threw his arms around him and kissed him.

The son said to him, 'Father, I have sinned against heaven and against you. I am no longer worthy to be called your son.'

But the father said to his servants, 'Quick! Bring the best robe and put it on him. Put a ring on his finger and sandals on his feet. Bring the fattened calf and kill it. Let's have a feast and celebrate. For this son of mine was dead and is alive again; he was lost and is found.' So they began to celebrate.

(Luke 15:11–24)

Within his culture, for the son to ask for his inheritance early was tantamount to wishing his father was already dead, and taken in its historical context perhaps the most surprising thing is that the old man did not lash out in anger at such an outrageous request. To be prodigal means to be generous to the point of recklessness, to give without concern for whether what is given will be wasted, and it seems to me that the father, in agreeing to give his son the inheritance, was at least as prodigal as his son. Although the son was not very smart in his choice of friends, it is worth pausing to consider that his unmerited generosity towards them was reminiscent of his father's open-handed approach.

The other notable feature of Luke's account is that the son did not come home to say sorry and restore the relationship, but simply in the hope of getting a roof over his head. It was his father who was interested in the restoration of the relationship, and once again his unstinting generosity came to the fore. It was considered humiliating in that culture for an elder to run, but the father, we are told, ran down the road towards his son, and met him before he ever arrived home – something which James Tissot's painting *The Return of the Prodigal Son* at least nods towards.

Søren Kierkegaard pointed out that the heart of the story is not the son's return, but the father's action of going out to look for him. The father does not wait inside his house for his son to come knocking on heaven's door, but goes out to find him – an action that is subsequently repeated towards the older son who, caught up in seething resentment, refuses to join in the welcome party and goes outside to sulk.

Meanwhile, the older son was in the field. When he came near the house, he heard music and dancing. So he called one of the servants and asked him what was going on. 'Your brother has come,' he replied, 'and your father has killed the fattened calf because he has him back safe and sound.'

The older brother became angry and refused to go in. So his father went out and pleaded with him. But he answered his father, 'Look! All these years I've been slaving for you and never disobeyed your orders. Yet you never gave me even a young goat so I could celebrate with my friends. But when this son of yours who has squandered your property with prostitutes comes home, you kill the fattened calf for him!'

'My son,' the father said, 'you are always with me, and everything I have is yours. But we had to celebrate

and be glad, because this brother of yours was
dead and is alive again; he was lost and is found.'

(Luke 15:25–32)

Both brothers, in the end, had failed to understand the
prodigal, outrageous, extravagant, unconditional love of the
father. You might even say that the parable would be better
titled 'the prodigal father'.

The parable has inspired countless works of art, including
The Prodigal Son (c. 1496) by Albrecht Dürer, and *The Return
of the Prodigal Son* (1773) by Pompeo Batoni. Both Rembrandt
and Gerard van Honthorst painted scenes of the prodigal
son's riotous life, and Rembrandt also painted *The Return of
the Prodigal Son*. The renowned author, professor and priest
Henri Nouwen was entranced by this painting, and it inspired
him to write a book on the parable in which he imagined
himself into each of the three roles – the two brothers and
the father.[10] The themes of the prodigal son are also played
out in Marilynne Robinson's novel *Home*, which artfully
explores the layers of complexity that the ongoing relationship would face after a son's homecoming. And it appears
often in music, such as in the Irish folk song 'The Wild
Rover', 'Prodigal Blues' by Billy Idol, and 'Prodigal Son' by
British heavy metal band Iron Maiden.

The sower

Van Gogh painted peasant figures over and over again, feeling drawn to the gnarled features and worn frames of people
who lived by hard physical work. But one theme he returned

to quite a number of times was inspired not only by rural life, but by the parable of the sower. It appears in Luke's and Mark's Gospels, as well as this version by Matthew:

> That same day Jesus went out of the house and sat by the lake. Such large crowds gathered around him that he got into a boat and sat in it, while all the people stood on the shore. Then he told them many things in parables, saying: 'A farmer went out to sow his seed. As he was scattering the seed, some fell along the path, and the birds came and ate it up. Some fell on rocky places, where it did not have much soil. It sprang up quickly, because the soil was shallow. But when the sun came up, the plants were scorched, and they withered because they had no root. Other seed fell among thorns, which grew up and choked the plants. Still other seed fell on good soil, where it produced a crop – a hundred, sixty or thirty times what was sown. Whoever has ears, let them hear.'
>
> (Matt. 13:1–9)

Van Gogh was born into a family of preachers and art dealers, and after a few years working in the art trade himself he became disillusioned with it as a soulless business, and came to the belief that his vocation was as a preacher. He read extensively, and spent many hours reading his Bible. He wrote in 1877 that a sermon on the parable of the sower had made a deep impression on him, and in another letter that he wanted to become a 'sower of the word'. He was not received into theological college, but he did get a position as an evangelist among the poor, and for a time he lived in very straitened circumstances in a mining district in Belgium.

Eventually he discovered his true vocation as a painter, but the experience of living among the poor remained with him and gave him the insight to paint such pictures as *The Potato Eaters*. And the parable of the sower remained an equally powerful image for him as a painter, just as much as it had when he was trying to be an evangelist. Several times he said that for him, making sketches and studies was like sowing, and making paintings and drawings later was reaping.

Van Gogh was a great admirer of Jean-François Millet, whose 'social realism' abandoned the romanticised image of the countryside in favour of painting working life in all its tough reality. Millet's *The Sower* (1850, Museum of Fine Arts, Boston) was a study of a solitary figure sowing by the old-fashioned method of throwing out armfuls of seed from a hand-held basket, and the painting is often seen as a metaphor for a new social justice being sown under the rising sun of a new era. Although he never saw Millet's painting in the original, Van Gogh found it moving and inspiring, and he worked his early pictures of the sower directly from Millet's image. His later versions still owed something to that early inspiration.

In all, Van Gogh made more than thirty paintings of *The Sower*, as well as a number of sketches. The early ones include such details as birds pecking up some of the seed, and a stony pathway where nothing grows. But his most enduring image of the sower, and the one he himself liked the best, was made shortly after he moved to Arles in 1888, by which time he had discovered some other influences to draw on.

In Paris, Van Gogh had collected and studied some late nineteenth-century Japanese coloured woodcuts, and became quite preoccupied not only with their aesthetic beauty, but also with the knowledge that they had been created in artists' communities. This fed his own dream of building an artists' collective in Provence. In September 1888 he wrote in a letter from Arles, 'I do not need Japanese things any more, since here I am in Japan.' A month later he painted *The Sower*, this time employing both the imagery and the brilliant colours of the woodcuts. The sky is painted in yellow and green, the field in shades of purple and blue, and the line of the picture is broken by a tree resembling a Japanese plum. The Japanese plum tree is a symbol of spring and new life, and is also used symbolically to stave off evil and misfortune.

The sower himself is silhouetted against the field, beneath a huge sun. Although sowing was usually a sunrise activity, some have argued that the painting is more suggestive of a sunset, and seen this way the imagery might connect the idea of a coming judgement that features in Matthew's version of the parable. This would certainly make sense in combination with the symbolism of the plum tree as a talisman against evil. Rising or setting, though, for Van Gogh the sun itself (and its reflected image in the sunflowers) was always a symbol of God's presence.

There is another, smaller painting of the sower from the same year, almost identical in theme and similar in colouring, and it would be easy to assume that the small one was a study for the larger painting. In fact, the smaller painting was a second version; Van Gogh was so pleased with his painting that almost immediately he set about repeating it, this time working more quickly, and using darker colours – the sky more green, the field a deep indigo.

⇌

Simon Peter

One of Jesus' disciples and closest friends who appears frequently in paintings, illuminated manuscripts and stained glass is Simon Peter (also known as St Peter). It was Peter to whom Jesus gave 'the keys of the kingdom', and who became the first leader of the early church. *The Calling of Peter and Andrew* (1308–11) by Duccio di Buoninsegna (c. 1255–1319) in the National Gallery of Art, Washington, shows Simon Peter in a boat with his brother, revealing his origins as a fisherman. The Gospels of Matthew, Mark and Luke divide Jesus' ministry roughly into two halves, the first half mostly in and around Galilee in the north of the country, and the second half tracing Jesus' travels en route to Jerusalem, where eventually he was put to death. The mid-point of the story takes place in Caesarea Philippi which, if you were travelling from Galilee to Jerusalem via the scenic route along the coast, is also roughly the halfway point geographically. And here Jesus asked his disciples a crucial question:

> Now when Jesus came into the district of Caesarea Philippi, he asked his disciples, 'Who do people say that the Son of Man is?' And they said, 'Some say John the Baptist, but others Elijah, and still others Jeremiah or one of the prophets.' He said to them, 'But who do you say that I am?' Simon Peter answered, 'You are the Messiah, the Son of the living God.' And Jesus

answered him, 'Blessed are you, Simon son of Jonah! For flesh and blood has not revealed this to you, but my Father in heaven. And I tell you, you are Peter, and on this rock I will build my church, and the gates of Hades will not prevail against it. I will give you the keys of the kingdom of heaven, and whatever you bind on earth will be bound in heaven, and whatever you loose on earth will be loosed in heaven.' Then he sternly ordered the disciples not to tell anyone that he was the Messiah.

(Matt. 16:13–20 NRSV)

This story is known as 'Peter's confession'. A number of paintings that depict this event show Jesus literally handing over a bunch of keys to Peter – for example, Pietro Perugino's *Christ Handing the Keys to St Peter* (Fresco, Sistine Chapel, Vatican), and Raphael's 1515 painting *The Handing-over the Keys* (Victoria and Albert Museum, London). Other paintings and stained-glass portraits often show a man who could be anyone except that a large pair of keys on his belt or in his hands, or simply in the margins of the picture, give the vital clue that it is Peter. And sometimes the figure of Peter is left out altogether and he is represented simply by a pair of crossed keys over an inverted crucifix because, according to tradition, St Peter was martyred upside down on a cross.

Precisely what the 'keys of the kingdom' originally meant is uncertain, but it quickly took on the tradition that St Peter stands at the door (or pearly gates) of heaven, monitoring admissions. He has also become the patron saint of keys, locks and security. These roles are summed up in a comical and affectionate description in Frank Cottrell Boyce's children's novel, *Millions*. Following the death of his mother, Damian, the nine-year-old protagonist, becomes obsessed with saints and has visions and conversations with a whole host of them. The saints are taken off their pedestals and portrayed as fully human, and when St Peter appears to Damian he describes himself as 'the patron saint of keys and locks and security arrangements in general'. He goes on to say, 'You're stressed. I'm stressed. We're all stressed. This is my portfolio, right – like I said, keys, locks, security. On top of that – fishermen, popes, Rome . . . I am run off my [swear] feet. I'm supposed to mind the gate too you know. I see everyone in and everyone out.'[11]

Jesus as mother

One of the criticisms often levelled at the Bible (and not without justification) is that it is patriarchal. But in the art and literature of the medieval era, God and Christ are often depicted as a mother, while also retaining male features.

A stained-glass window in St Mark's Church, Gillingham, Kent, shows a mother pelican feeding her young. According to medieval folklore, the pelican had the deepest of maternal instincts and it was believed that if she had no food to give to her chicks, she would peck her own breast and feed them with her own blood. For this reason the female pelican became an icon of Jesus, feeding his Church with his own body and blood through the ritual of the Eucharist (Holy Communion).

There are medieval paintings, which appear very strange to the modern eye, of Jesus hanging on a cross while breast-feeding the Church. This is effectively a combination of the idea that the sacrifice of Jesus both saves and feeds his followers. The metaphor of God as a mother appears in the prophets. In Isaiah God says:

> For a long time I have held my peace,
> I have kept still and restrained myself;
> now I will cry out like a woman in labour,
> I will gasp and pant.
>
> (Isa. 42:14 NRSV)

Less difficult to grasp are some of the poems and prose of the medieval era that simply elaborate on the idea of the motherhood of God, a primary example being the writing of Julian of Norwich, who was unusual not only for being an early female author, but also for writing in English:

> [Christ] Our natural mother, our gracious mother, because he willed to become our mother in everything, took the ground for his work most humbly and most mildly in the maiden's womb . . . Our high God, the sovereign wisdom of all, arrayed himself in this low place and made himself entirely ready in our poor flesh in order to do the service and the office of motherhood himself in all things.
>
> . . . A mother can give her child milk to suck, but our precious mother, Jesus, can feed us with himself. He does so most courteously and most tenderly, with the Blessed Sacrament, which is the precious food of true life. With all the sweet sacraments he sustains us most mercifully and graciously. That is what he meant in these blessed words, where he said, 'I am that which

holy Church preaches and teaches you,' that is to say, 'All the health and life of the sacraments, all the virtue and grace of my word, all the goodness that is ordained for you in holy Church, that I am.'[12]

To view Jesus in this way seems comforting and inspiring to some people who see Christianity as predominantly an aggressively male and patriarchal system. To others it seems strange, even a little tortured, to portray Jesus as both feminine and masculine.

Mary Magdalene

By the standards of the time in which they were written, some parts of the New Testament give women a surprisingly prominent place. Luke's Gospel in particular gives quite a lot of attention to Jesus' interaction with the women among his followers, one of the most famous being Mary Magdalene, about whom there is at least as much legend as fact.

Mary Magdalene is only mentioned a few times in the Gospels, mostly towards the end of the story. She followed Jesus on his journey to Jerusalem, stayed loyally beside him while he died, and was the first to witness his resurrection. Both the significance of her actions and the intrigue surrounding her identity gradually turned her into a major figure in Christianity.

For centuries it was commonly thought that Mary was a prostitute, although the Gospels do not actually say this. We first meet her in Luke's Gospel:

After this, Jesus travelled about from one town and village to another, proclaiming the good news of the kingdom of God. The Twelve were with him, and also some women who had been cured of evil spirits and diseases: Mary (called Magdalene) from whom seven demons had come out; Joanna the wife of Chuza, the manager of Herod's household; Susanna; and many others. These women were helping to support them out of their own means.

(Luke 8:1–3)

'Cured of evil spirits' is most likely to have meant some sort of mental illness or anxiety, and the fact that Mary had seven demons suggests that she was very badly afflicted. But her legendary status as a reformed prostitute is unrelated to this, and seems to have come about through the conflation of two similar stories of women who came to Jesus during his journey and wept at his feet. One of these, which occurs immediately before Mary's first appearance, is about a woman whose name is not mentioned, but who 'lived a sinful life'. She fell at Jesus' feet weeping, and then wiped the tears away with her long hair. The fact that she had not tied up her hair in public was a cultural clue that this woman was a prostitute – but although this account appears just before the first mention of Mary and her seven demons, Luke does not say that it was the same woman. A similar story appears in John 12, where Jesus stayed in Bethany with some friends, Lazarus and his sisters Martha and Mary. On this occasion, Mary of Bethany takes a sizeable alabaster jar of pure nard – the essential ingredient in the most expensive perfume, something of a very high value that would have represented her financial security – and used this to anoint Jesus' feet. This act took on a religious symbolism, because nard was an ingredient used both in temple worship and in anointing kings for their death (a jar with traces of nard was found in the tomb of Tutankhamun). So this was a sign that Jesus was, in the religious sense, being worshipped as a god and being anointed for a royal burial. But having anointed his feet, Mary of Bethany then wiped his feet with her hair.

The two stories of women weeping at Jesus' feet, one of whom was a prostitute and the other called Mary, were confused. In a sermon preached in AD 591, Pope Gregory the Great stated that the woman in both stories was Mary Magdalene, confirming the legend that she was a prostitute, and since then she has been painted, sculpted and eulogised as the example of a fallen woman restored. Paintings of Mary often show her with long flowing red hair, or dressed in scarlet 'come-and-get-me' clothes.

Caravaggio's 1597 portrait *The Penitent Magdalene* presents Mary not as a common prostitute, but as a rich courtesan in fine clothes and again the flowing red hair, but kneeling to pray and with her jewellery thrown to the ground beside her, looking for all the world like a woman tired of life. Other depictions show her in her restored state, dressed respectably, hair covered, reading quietly in a corner, and due to the confusion of the two Marys, Mary Magdalene's image often appears with an alabaster perfume jar, such as Piero di Cosimo's *St Mary Magdalene* (1490s, Galleria Nazionale d'Arte Antica, Rome), where Mary appears as the ideal Renaissance woman, seated serenely at a table and reading, with the ornate jar beside her.

It was not until 1969 that the Second Vatican Council

officially stated that Mary of Magdalene and the unnamed sinner were two different figures. But by this time Mary's name had long been associated with the tragic abuses of the Magdalene Laundries – institutions attached to convents where 'fallen' girls were sent, often for their entire lives, locked away from the outside world to work long hours in hot, steamy laundries, which became a metaphor for washing away their 'sins'. As often as not the girls were the victims of abuse, orphans, or merely deemed to be in moral danger because they were attractive. It is shocking to realise that the last of the Magdalene institutions was closed only in the 1990s. This outrage was documented in Peter Mullan's 2002 film, *The Magdalene Sisters*, but the story is told from the point of view of the girls themselves by Joni Mitchell in her 1994 song, 'The Magdalene Laundries'[13]. The song is deeply poignant, expressing the dull hopelessness of girls who arrived there pregnant through incest or abuse, only to realise they would spend the rest of their days in the laundry, washing until their hands were chapped and bleeding. The fact that Mary Magdalene's story was about forgiveness, justice and restoration was entirely lost in this inhumane regime.

There are two main legends about what happened to Mary Magdalene after Jesus' death, although there is no historical data to support either of them. The Eastern Church holds that she travelled with Mary the mother of Jesus to Ephesus, in modern-day Turkey, but Western tradition is that she went to southern France and lived for thirty years as a hermit in a cave. This is why she sometimes appears as old, ragged and underfed, such as in Donatello's sculpture (1455) in the

Duomo Museum, Florence, or the panel *St John the Baptist, Mary Magdalene* by Filippino Lippi (c. 1500, Galleria dell'Accademia, Florence), in which the two emaciated saints are shown as examples of mortification of the flesh. Here, too, Mary is shown with flowing red hair.

Jesus Christ Superstar, the 1970s musical by Tim Rice and Andrew Lloyd Webber, blurred these different ideas, depicting Mary not necessarily as a prostitute, but as a girl with many lovers who then finds herself disarmed by the quality of power, love and friendship she encounters in Jesus. Mary's song 'I Don't Know How To Love Him' left the question hanging in the air as to quite what her relationship was with Jesus.

Just as there is no evidence in the Gospels for Mary being a prostitute, neither is there any evidence for the claim that she was Jesus' wife. Mary is associated with various mystic and Gnostic accounts of Christianity, one of which is entitled *The Gnostic Gospel of Mary*. These have provided the backbone for some popular fiction, and include the myth that lies behind *The Da Vinci Code* by Dan Brown, in which Mary became pregnant with Jesus' child, and her descendants founded the Merovingian line of kings.

An idea that has been floated more recently is that Mary was one of Jesus' leading disciples, but that her status was kept in the shadows in the written record because it was not considered a woman's place to be a religious leader. A figure who appears repeatedly in John's Gospel is simply called 'the disciple whom Jesus loved', and by tradition this is thought to have been John himself. But one or two scholars have recently suggested that this disciple was actually Mary Magdalene, associating the idea with Da Vinci's painting of the Last Supper, in which the disciple whom Jesus loved, sitting at his right hand, appears to be feminine. Some have even suggested that Mary might have been the author behind John's Gospel, and although the theory has gained little currency, it is interesting to notice that in a world where a rescued prostitute is no longer considered sensational, once again Mary Magdalene becomes the hook on which to hang a current controversy – this time, the pressing question as to where the women were who have never been given their due in the records of history.

The little that the Gospels themselves tell of Mary Magdalene is that she was a faithful follower of Jesus, the first person to see him after the resurrection, and the first 'evangelist' or teller of the gospel. The controversy and legend that has surrounded her since is mostly invented to fill the gaps in the story of this iconic and controversial woman.

9
Betrayed with a kiss

Jesus Christ was about thirty-three years old when he was put to death by crucifixion. The last week of his life, and the events that immediately followed, were of such enormous significance for his followers that since Christianity established itself as the predominant religion in European culture, the events of that week have been portrayed countless times in art, music, literature and poetry.

The Gospels relate that Jesus and his disciples had travelled south to Jerusalem for the great feast of the Passover. The atmosphere was pretty charged for a whole set of reasons. Palestine was under Roman occupation, and as taxes rose so did the social tensions. Meanwhile, Jesus was drawing a sizeable following wherever he went. In the twenty-first century, Jesus is associated almost entirely with religion, but in his own time those who followed him expected that he would be just as much a political liberator as a religious saviour – in fact it is probably true that for many people the two ideas were practically inseparable. But like most popular and famous people, he was not universally liked. There is no single clear reason why Jesus' enemies wanted him out of the way, but it seems that there were some who feared that he would lead an uprising, and others who resented his popularity, and it was not long before events turned against him.

The way the Gospels tell it, Jesus could see that he was walking into the face of danger, and believed that it was his fate. But in practical terms, the beginning of the end was the betrayal of Jesus by his friend and disciple Judas Iscariot, whose name has become the by-word for betrayal. Judas had been one of Jesus' closest friends and disciples for three years. Some believe that he became disillusioned when he realised that Jesus was not going to bring them political liberation; others think that, as the group's treasurer, it was potential riches that turned his head. But whatever the motive, once they arrived in Jerusalem, Judas accepted a bribe of thirty pieces of silver from Jesus' enemies to hand him over to his death.

The betrayal took place on the last night of Jesus' freedom. Together with Judas and the other disciples, Jesus ate supper with his friends – a meal that has been immortalised as the Last Supper, and painted dozens of times. Traditionally in Last Supper scenes Judas is separated from the group in some way, to symbolise the fact that he is about to betray Jesus.

An unusually well-preserved twelfth-century passion fresco in Ickleton Church, Cambridgeshire, shows Judas on the opposite side of the table from the others. He is in the same position in Castagno's *Last Supper* (c. 1450), a fresco at the Sant'Apollonia Convent in Florence, and here the symbolism is heightened by his face resembling a satyr, an ancient symbol of evil. In Leonardo da Vinci's *Last Supper* (1495–8), which is a wall painting rather than a true fresco, Judas is seated among the disciples, but a shadow is cast across his face. In just a few examples, Judas is shown underneath the table. A Romanesque stone carving over the door of the village church at Neuilly-en-Donjon, France, shows Judas crouched underneath the table, and John Piper copied this unusual format in his small stained-glass window *The Beginning and the End* in the side chapel of Robinson College, Cambridge.

The Gospels record that towards the end of the supper, Judas slipped out into the night, and Jesus then went out to pray in the garden of Gethsemane. There Judas brought a group of guards with him, having pre-arranged with them that he would identify Jesus with a kiss. Had Judas been an Englishman, he would have shaken Jesus by the hand, but in his culture the standard greeting was the kiss of friendship. As the guards moved to arrest Jesus, Simon Peter stepped forward and cut off the ear of one of the guards (John 18:10), and paintings of Gethsemane sometimes include this detail.

The story of Judas has been told in popular songs for centuries. An English folk song from the thirteenth century is reproduced in *The Oxford Book of Ballads*, retelling it as a simple narrative,[1] whereas U2's song 'Judas' imagines the turmoil of regret and memories that Judas might have experienced as he slowly drove himself to his own death. But not all depictions of Judas accept the interpretation that he betrayed Jesus and therefore was a villain. In his 1964 anti-war song 'With God on Our Side', Bob Dylan uses the conundrum of Judas's act of betrayal, and the possibility that Judas himself might have been motivated by a sense that he was doing the right thing, to underline his protest that nations going to war nearly always assume that their actions are justified, either by God or just because they have the moral high ground. The idea that Judas was part of some kind of secret plot or conspiracy has been floated elsewhere, such as in the controversy that arose over a Gnostic text called *The Gospel of Judas*. One translation seemed to suggest that Judas might have been set up to betray Jesus, but like most conspiracy theories surrounding the Bible, it did not prove to have credibility or dramatically alter people's perception of Judas. It seems that Judas's story remains as one of love, betrayal, loss, grief and despair, and that being 'sold for thirty pieces of silver' will continue to be shorthand for a cheap betrayal.

Crucifixion

In 1975 about a thousand delegates gathered at the Nairobi Assembly of the World Council of Churches. For nearly ten years, the WCC had been working on projects to combat racism and political oppression, and this theme was given a great deal of attention at the 1975 gathering. Many of the delegates – those from Latin America, Asia, Africa and Eastern Europe – had themselves been the victims of crushing oppression.

At the opening of the Nairobi Assembly, there was displayed in one of the central public spaces a sculpture by Brazilian artist Guido Rocha. *The Tortured Christ* showed a life-size, emaciated Jesus hanging on a cross, every sinew stretched in agony, his eyes screwed up and his mouth wide open as he screamed in pain, anguish and rage. Rocha had, reportedly, been a victim of torture himself at one time, and his sculpture showed graphically the kind of unbearable agony that Christ would have endured. And by giving his figure of Christ Brazilian features, there was a strong sense of identity. This was not a far-off God, but a Christ who is 'one of us'.

The sculpture, though, had such a disturbing impact on the delegates that after a couple of days the WCC leaders felt they had to move it out of its very public position and put it in a basement room so that people had to go out of their way to view it. The very act of moving it caused just as much controversy as the sculpture itself, as many people found it incongruous that Christians attending a conference devoted to addressing issues of racism, injustice, apartheid and oppression could not bear to look at an image of the dying Christ that was a touch too realistic.

Rocha's work was in stark contrast to more familiar images of Christ's death. Take, for instance, *Christ on the Cross* by Diego Velazquez (1632, Museo del Prado, Madrid). Like the Rocha sculpture, it is a life-size portrait of the crucified Christ, and this, too, was intended to give a realistic picture. Velazquez painted it after he returned from his first trip to Italy. Having grown up familiar with the mannerism of the Italian High Renaissance, where figures were painted in carefully set-up poses and surrounded by flowers, pillars, buildings and animals, all laden with symbolic meanings, Velazquez began to move away from this stylised form and to paint in a simpler, naturalistic way. Certainly by comparison with Mannerist crucifixions, Velazquez's Jesus seems simple and untheatrical. Yet to the modern eye what is most striking is that Jesus seems to be dying very calmly, with an air of sadness but without serious distress. This Christ is serene and spiritual, and in control even of his death.

As striking as both these works are in their own right, they are so dramatically different that they beg the question: which artist gets closer to the biblical account? The answer, strangely enough, is that they both do – because the different versions of the story told by the evangelists are every bit as different as these two works of art.

As often as not, Jesus' death is remembered as an amalgamation of all the various bits of the story from the four Gospels. But while combining the accounts may satisfy a need for completeness, what is lost is the particular characterisation and stress that each Gospel writer sought to give. Mark's account of the death of Jesus is brief and to the point, with the immediacy of a reporter at the scene talking to camera. Mark's Jesus seems very human, and as he dies a brutal death you can almost feel the pain. Luke's account has Jesus speaking words of comfort to all those around him as he dies, but Mark does not mention any words of forgiveness or concern for his friends, just one final agonised cry of dereliction: 'My God, my God, why have you forsaken me?' (Mark 15:34).

> It was nine in the morning when they crucified him. The written notice of the charge against him read: THE KING OF THE JEWS. They crucified two rebels with him, one on his right and one on his left. Those who passed by hurled insults at him, shaking their heads and saying, 'So! You who are going to destroy the temple and build it in three days, come down from the cross and save yourself!'

In the same way the chief priests and the teachers of the law mocked him among themselves. 'He saved others,' they said, 'but he can't save himself! Let this Messiah, this king of Israel, come down now from the cross, that we may see and believe.' Those crucified with him also heaped insults on him.

At noon, darkness came over the whole land until three in the afternoon. And at three in the afternoon Jesus cried out in a loud voice, '*Eloi, Eloi, lema sabachthani?*' (which means 'My God, my God, why have you forsaken me?').

When some of those standing near heard this, they said, 'Listen, he's calling Elijah.'

Someone ran, filled a sponge with wine vinegar, put it on a staff, and offered it to Jesus to drink. 'Now leave him alone. Let's see if Elijah comes to take him down,' he said.

With a loud cry, Jesus breathed his last.

(Mark 15:25–37)

By contrast, John, who began his Gospel 'In the beginning . . .' and gave the sense that every detail of Jesus' life was deliberate and part of God's plan from eternity to eternity, shows Jesus calmly in control of events even to the moment of his death. Luke reported that Simon of Cyrene carried Jesus' cross for him. But John's Jesus carries his own cross, spends the final hours of his death talking calmly to his friends, and when the moment comes he seems eventually to relinquish his life, rather than having it torn from him.

Carrying his own cross, he went out to the place of the Skull (which in Aramaic is called Golgotha). Here they crucified him, and with him two others – one on each side and Jesus in the middle . . .

Near the cross of Jesus stood his mother, his mother's sister, Mary the wife of Clopas, and Mary Magdalene. When Jesus saw his mother there, and the disciple whom he loved standing nearby, he said to her, 'Woman, here is your son,' and to the disciple, 'Here is your mother.' From that time on, this disciple took her into his home.

Later, knowing that everything had now been finished, and so that Scripture would be fulfilled, Jesus said, 'I am thirsty.' A jar of wine vinegar was there, so they soaked a sponge in it, put the sponge on a stalk of the hyssop plant, and lifted it to Jesus' lips. When he had received the drink, Jesus said, 'It is finished.' With that, he bowed his head and gave up his spirit.

(John 19:17–18, 25–30)

Like the two works of art, the different Gospel accounts show clearly that the death of Christ did not have just one meaning and interpretation. For Rocha, as for St Mark, the spotlight is on the theological idea that Christ came to be one of us – not just God near us, or among us, but quite literally one of us. Jesus was thoroughly human, as well as divine – he was not just God wearing a human body like a suit of clothes, but real flesh and blood. John, though, seemed to put the focus on another strand of theology – that Jesus was not destroyed by death, but triumphed over it.

Another work of art that was created to make the crucifixion 'real' to its viewers is an Anglo-Saxon cross, known as the Ruthwell Cross, that stands in Ruthwell Church, Dumfriesshire, Scotland. This cross is covered in carved images showing scenes from the death and resurrection of Christ, and around its edges, in runes, an old poem is inscribed.

> Christ was on the cross, and there hastening from afar came they to the noble prince. I that all beheld. With missiles wounded, they laid him down limb-weary, they stood at his body's head.

In this case, the poem is narrated by the cross itself, and the effect is that the cross speaks to the reader as if it was an eye-witness to the event and shared in Christ's agony, and has survived to tell the tale, making a link in time and space between Christ and the reader.[2]

The crucifixion is such a central and familiar image in art that its traditional meanings can be completely subverted to become a hook on which to hang new ideas – Damien Hirst and Craigie Aitchison being two artists who have given the crucifixion unconventional treatments. And Banksy, the renowned graffiti artist, painted a *Christ with Shopping Bags* – the familiar shape of Christ with outstretched arms and a halo, and with dripping paint representing the bloody tragedy of the image. But in Christ's hands are seven or eight shopping bags, the kind of bags you get from smart shops, tied with ribbon. *Christ with Shopping Bags* seems to comment on the way in which consumerism has become so central to Western culture that it is, in a sense, the 'worship' of the age. With the shopping centre as the new cathedral, have we become so shallow that shopping is now our object of worship? And are we even aware of what it is really costing us?

It is impossible, then, to say which image is closest to the truth; each image, like each Gospel writer, draws out different elements and interpretations. You might find a confluence of ideas between Mark's Gospel and the sheer agony of Guido Rocha's tortured image, or the tragedy and isolation that Craigie Aitchison conveys in his figures of a Christ with no arms. On the other hand, you can look at any of these images and see that each of them, however near or far it seems to be to the historical narrative, becomes a Midrash on the story, asking what the crucifixion says to us now. While for some it will retain some of its traditional religious meaning, for others it might ask whether there are matters of supreme value that, simply by taking them for granted, or by our inaction, we are allowing to be put to death right under our noses. Perhaps the power of Banksy's image will wake us up to the mindlessness of consumer culture and call us to something greater, or Rocha's might launch us into action on behalf of those who endure intolerable suffering.

Pietà

It was late on 8 July 1984. It had been a perfect summer's day, and the evening was warm and close. Bob Littlewood, York Minster's Superintendent of Works, was enjoying the scene from his window as spectacular forks of summer light-ning split the sky over the Yorkshire landscape.

Not long after midnight, Mr Littlewood received a call to say that the Minster's fire alarm had been set off. False alarms were not unusual, so he was calm as he made his way to the Minster. But to his dismay he arrived to see flames licking the roof of the South Transept. It was soon discovered that the fire had started at the only entrance to the roof void, making it impossible to get directly to the seat of the fire, and it was a couple of hours before the roof collapsed and the blaze was brought under control. But by this time enor-mous damage had been done to the Minster from the fire, the falling beams, and the thousands of gallons of water that had been used to extinguish the flames.

No one knows how the fire started; it may well have been a lightning strike. But the story quickly spread that the fire was an act of divine retribution, because the newly appointed Bishop of Durham had made various controversial comments on national radio about the resurrection, the virgin birth and other 'miraculous' ideas.

Ironically, though, in the aftermath of the fire, it seemed that a minor miracle had taken place – for, as the rose window burned that night in 1984, another far more fragile work of art survived intact, against all the odds, only a few feet from the blaze. When the burnt timbers were cleared away, Fenwick Lawson's huge driftwood sculpture of the *Pietà* was found, slightly scorched but otherwise unharmed. And while the York fire was a sad sight to see, the *Pietà* depicts a human catastrophe that is beyond words to express.

The *Pietà* (which in Italian means 'pity') is more often seen in sculpture than in painting, and shows the mother of Jesus cradling the dead body of her son after he is removed from the cross. The *Pietà* tradition seems to have originated in northern Europe, and most medieval depictions of the scene display raw human emotion just as much as theological symbolism, although earlier ones tended to be more controlled, showing Mary as immovable, by contrast with the disciples, most of whom ran away at the first sight of danger.

Some say that Michelangelo's famous marble *Pietà* shows the grief of God himself reflected in the face of Mary, making Mary symbolic of the divine response to the death of Christ. Lawson's sculpture, though, captures in the figure of Mary the mix of heartbreak and stunned disbelief that people often experience in the face of violent and traumatic death.

Photograph by Paul Judson. Used with permission

It is hard to imagine anything more unbearable than the death of one's own child, and the agony of human loss is written all over this sculpture. Lawson depicts scenes of political injustice as often as he does religious subjects, and he always lets the character of the wood he works with shape what he makes. Here as Mary looks down at the body of her son, her face is riven with two huge cracks and several smaller ones. The small cracks seem to paint tears onto her face, while the large cracks that extend right down her upper body seem to describe the depth of despairing grief that makes you feel as if you are literally coming to pieces. The figures are made from driftwood, which adds a sense of fragility and ordinary humanity, and of all the biblical titles given to Jesus, he is here more than anything 'a man of sorrows' and 'acquainted with grief' (Isa. 53:3). 'Surely he took up our pain and bore our suffering,' wrote Isaiah (53:4), a description that seems better executed in battered driftwood than polished oak.

Although the *Pietà* is a common image in sculpture and painting, it is not drawn directly from the Gospels, but is a development of a scene known either as the 'Deposition' (the removal of the body from the cross) or the 'Lamentation', which shows Mary and various disciples grieving over the body of Christ before he is put in the tomb. A Deposition or Lamentation is the thirteenth of fourteen 'Stations of the Cross', a tradition that developed through medieval pilgrims walking in the footsteps of Christ on the last day of his life, from his trial to his burial. The fourteen stations can be seen depicted around the walls of many Catholic churches. It is thought that the *Pietà* may have emerged from the Stations of the Cross, and as such it is an imaginative depiction of what might have happened. But John's Gospel does record that Mary was present at the crucifixion:

> Near the cross of Jesus stood his mother, his mother's sister, Mary the wife of Clopas, and Mary Magdalene. When Jesus saw his mother there, and the disciple whom he loved standing nearby, he said to her, 'Woman, here is your son,' and to the disciple, 'Here is your mother.' From that time on, this disciple took her into his home.
>
> (John 19:25–7)

The final act of Jesus, according to John, was to take care of his own mother, who was already a widow and was now losing her eldest son. The plight of the widow in first-century Palestine was pretty bleak: if her husband died, all his property would revert to his family and not to her, so she would have been utterly dependent on the mercy of her in-laws, or of other charitable friends and neighbours. For Mary to lose first a husband and then a son was not only a personal tragedy, it was also an economic disaster. So asking John, his closest friend, to take Mary in as if she were his own mother was not merely sentimental but utterly practical in terms of taking care of Mary's daily needs.

The same scene is described in the *Stabat Mater*, a thirteenth-century poem that reflects both on Mary's sorrow and on her faithfulness and strength to the bitter end, as she stands at the foot of the cross.

Stabat Mater dolorosa iuxta crucem lacrimosa, dum pendebat Filius. Cuius animam gementem contrista- tam et dolentem pertransivit gladius.

The grieving mother stood weeping by the cross where her son was hanging. A sword passed through her weeping, kind and grieving soul.

Stabat Mater is sometimes seen to emphasise the idea of Mary's strength. The word 'stood' here means something more than 'not sitting' – it has the sense of staying, being stable, stand- ing up for something, refusing to give in. The *Stabat Mater* has been set to music dozens of times down the centuries, from early composers Palestrina and Charpentier, through the very famous settings by Pergolesi and Verdi, and most recently by jazz-influenced composer Karl Jenkins. The refer- ence to the sword picks up another detail from John's Gospel:

Now it was the day of Preparation, and the next day was to be a special Sabbath. Because the Jewish lead- ers did not want the bodies left on the crosses during the Sabbath, they asked Pilate to have the legs broken and the bodies taken down. The soldiers therefore came and broke the legs of the first man who had been crucified with Jesus, and then those of the other. But when they came to Jesus and found that he was already dead, they did not break his legs. Instead, one of the soldiers pierced Jesus' side with a spear, bringing a sudden flow of blood and water.

(John 19:31–4)

Elevated as he was on the cross, they could not check his breathing, but putting a sword through Jesus' side was a quick and crude way of checking that he was really dead. John records this detail because it connects the crucifixion of Jesus with the Passover sacrifice. 'Not one of his bones will be broken' appears in Exodus 12:46 and Numbers 9:12 as an instruction not to break the legs of an animal who would be sacrificed at Passover to atone for sin. The phrase also appears in Psalm 34:20, a poem about God's protection of the righteous, and 'They will look on me, the one they have pierced' are words about God himself that appear in the prophet Zechariah (12:10). Theologically, then, this confirms Jesus as the divine and righteous Son of God, and his death as an atonement for sin. But on a more human level it also recalls the story of the *Nunc Dimittis*, where the old prophet Simeon told Mary, only days after Jesus was born, that her conviction that Jesus was destined for extraordinary things would come at a cost. 'A sword shall pierce your heart,' said Simeon to Mary. In the moment of Jesus death, as the sword pierced his side, surely Mary must have felt as if her own soul had been cut into pieces.

Within a religious context the *Pietà* and the *Stabat Mater* both show Mary as an example of spirituality for others to follow – especially when she is shown as serenely faithful. But this can hide the fact that behind the religious and theological significance was a completely human experience. One of the reasons I like Fenwick Lawson's sculpture is because it captures the humanity of Mary and Jesus, and the raw reality of the tragic events that happened some two thousand years ago to a group of people not so very different from us.

Resurrection

The strange story of Jesus' resurrection has been given many different interpretations by those trying to make sense of what 'really' happened. Some have argued that for the resurrection to mean anything at all, Jesus must quite literally have died and come back to life. Others have given it a more mystical explanation, saying that its importance is in the understanding that we are freed from living under what St Paul calls the 'law of death' and that the quality and reality of spiritual life is the real issue.

It would be a mistake, though, to imagine that the resurrection was taken literally before the modern era, and has only been challenged since the advent of the modern, scientific age. Even in the first few weeks after the death of Jesus, reactions to news of his resurrection varied just as much as they do today. But whatever interpretation you put on it, the resurrection has inspired some fantastic art, literature and music over the centuries, drawing out endless explorations of doubt and grief, or of transforming hope in the face of death and despair.

> Early on the first day of the week, while it was still dark, Mary Magdalene went to the tomb and saw that the stone had been removed from the entrance. So she came running to Simon Peter and the other disciple, the one Jesus loved, and said, 'They have taken the Lord out of the tomb, and we don't know where they have put him!'
>
> So Peter and the other disciple started for the

tomb. Both were running, but the other disciple outran Peter and reached the tomb first. He bent over and looked in at the strips of linen lying there but did not go in. Then Simon Peter came along behind him and went straight into the tomb. He saw the strips of linen lying there, as well as the cloth that had been wrapped around Jesus' head. The cloth was still lying in its place, separate from the linen. Finally the other disciple, who had reached the tomb first, also went inside. He saw and believed. (They still did not understand from Scripture that Jesus had to rise from the dead.) Then the disciples went back to where they were staying.

Now Mary stood outside the tomb crying. As she wept, she bent over to look into the tomb and saw two angels in white, seated where Jesus' body had been, one at the head and the other at the foot.

They asked her, 'Woman, why are you crying?'

'They have taken my Lord away,' she said, 'and I don't know where they have put him.' At this, she turned round and saw Jesus standing there, but she did not realise that it was Jesus.

He asked her, 'Woman, why are you crying? Who is it you are looking for?'

Thinking he was the gardener, she said, 'Sir, if you have carried him away, tell me where you have put him, and I will get him.'

Jesus said to her, 'Mary.'

She turned toward him and cried out in Aramaic, 'Rabboni!' (which means 'Teacher').

Jesus said, 'Do not hold on to me, for I have not

yet ascended to the Father. Go instead to my brothers and tell them, "I am ascending to my Father and your Father, to my God and your God."'

Mary Magdalene went to the disciples with the news: 'I have seen the Lord!' And she told them that he had said these things to her.

(John 20:1–18)

Gian Girolamo Savoldo painted *Mary Magdalene Approaching the Tomb* between 1535 and 1540. The centre of the painting is a study of Mary, who is crouched near the tomb, and on the left of the picture dawn is breaking on the horizon. But while Mary's body faces away from the viewer, she is looking back over her shoulder so that her face is clearly visible to the viewer, and she appears to be transfixed by something that is behind the viewer – so much so that you almost want to turn round yourself and see what she is looking at. Most striking of all is the fact that her face is lit up by a light much stronger than the breaking dawn, so that her face and her clothes seem to glow. The viewer, of course, is supposed to conclude that the light emanates from the resurrected Jesus.

Supper at Emmaus

St Luke tells the story of two disciples who, on the Sunday after Jesus' death, were walking to Emmaus, thought to be a village some six or seven miles outside Jerusalem. Along the way they encountered a stranger who walked along with them, and the three men talked about the death of Jesus.

The stranger began to explain to the disciples that the death was foretold in the Scriptures. Arriving at Emmaus, the disciples asked the stranger to stay for supper. Only when the stranger broke the bread at the table did this characteristic gesture make them recognise him.

The Italian painter Caravaggio (1571–1610) painted two different versions of *Supper at Emmaus* – one from 1601 is in the National Gallery in London, and another from 1606 is at the Brera Fine Arts Academy in Milan. Caravaggio was probably born in Milan, and his brief but brilliant painting career really took off when he arrived in Rome at the age of twenty. There he achieved huge success as a painter, and also got into a great deal of trouble because of his volatile temper. As a painter of the human form he was a virtuoso, rejecting the rather lifeless figures of Mannerism in favour of painting from life. His figures are full of vitality and feeling, and his scenes were made all the more dramatic through his use of chiaroscuro – a strong contrast between light and darkness. Among his paintings there are several that portray the stories of the resurrection, his dramatic touch bringing to life the expressions of amazement and disbelief on the disciples' faces.

Caravaggio's two versions of *Supper at Emmaus* are similar in composition; both show Christ at the centre breaking the bread, with a disciple at either side of the table in that split second of recognition. In the earlier version, their realisation of Christ's identity is emphasised by the brilliant light on his pale and beardless face, the light further accentuated by the bright white tablecloth and the dark shadow that falls behind him. The disciples' amazement is shown in their exaggerated poses. You can almost hear the sharp intake of breath and the scraping of the chair on the floor as one throws his hands out to his sides and the other starts to his feet. The man waiting at the table seems attentive and intrigued, presumably not understanding what is happening. The 1606 version is more restrained in every way. The colour is less bright, the contrast between light and dark a little less stark, and the expression of the disciples is more of a dawning realisation than a sudden leaping to their feet. In this version there are two figures waiting at the table, the innkeeper who seems only mildly interested, and his wife who looks so weary that she barely notices the disciples' reaction to Jesus, again making this seem more of a private recognition than the earlier version.

Doubting Thomas

St John's Gospel tells of several more resurrection appearances, including the story of Thomas, the disciple who was not present when the resurrected Jesus first appeared to his gathered disciples, and declared that unless he saw with his own eyes, he would not believe.

> Now Thomas (also known as Didymus), one of the Twelve, was not with the disciples when Jesus came. So the other disciples told him, 'We have seen the Lord!'
> But he said to them, 'Unless I see the nail marks in his hands and put my finger where the nails were, and put my hand into his side, I will not believe.'
> A week later his disciples were in the house again,

and Thomas was with them. Though the doors were locked, Jesus came and stood among them and said, 'Peace be with you!' Then he said to Thomas, 'Put your finger here; see my hands. Reach out your hand and put it into my side. Stop doubting and believe.'

Thomas said to him, 'My Lord and my God!'

Then Jesus told him, 'Because you have seen me, you have believed; blessed are those who have not seen and yet have believed.'

(John 20:24–9)

Thomas and Didymus are Aramaic and Greek for 'twin', but traditionally Thomas has been known as Doubting Thomas – a title that is hardly a compliment. But there is good reason, I think, for applauding Thomas, and a more deserving title would be 'Honest Thomas'. He seems to come off the page as a man of integrity who would rather put up with being the odd one out among his friends than fake his own beliefs.

In religious language, doubt is not the same thing as unbelief. Unbelief is a determined refusal to believe, whereas doubt indicates that faith, like knowledge, is always incomplete and open to question. In Judaism, according to Jonathan Sacks, the Chief Rabbi of Britain and the Commonwealth, 'To be without questions is not a sign of faith, but of lack of depth. We ask questions not because we doubt, but because we believe.'[3] Samuel Taylor Coleridge, best known as one of the Lakeland poets, was steeped in the Bible and wrote of how he had read it many times with great care. In the Bible, said Coleridge, 'there is more that finds me than I have experienced in all other books together; the words of the Bible find me at greater depths of my being'.[4]

Coleridge believed that for faith to be genuine, and not just a fantasy for the gullible, it was essential to grapple with doubt. 'Dubious questioning,' he wrote, 'is a much better evidence than that senseless deadness which most take for believing. People that know nothing have no doubts. Never be afraid to doubt, if only you have the disposition to believe, and doubt in order that you may end in believing the truth.'[5]

John's Gospel says that Christ invited Thomas to scrutinise his wounds, but it seems it was enough for Thomas simply to see Jesus standing before him. Immediately he knelt in worship before his Lord. But those who have portrayed Thomas in painting have usually shown him peering at the wound in Jesus' side. Caravaggio's *Doubting Thomas* (1602–3, Sanssouci, Potsdam) shows Thomas with a finger inside the wound, and John Granville Gregory's *Still Doubting*, which is based on Caravaggio's painting but relocated in a contemporary setting, shows Thomas dressed in a black leather coat, with little John Lennon glasses and an intelligent face – maybe a journalist, a scientist or even a detective? What Gregory himself intended by the painting is hard to judge, but it has triggered a range of responses from its viewers. Some have read into it that the sceptic may search for forensic evidence but will never believe; some have seen in it an affirmation that God will stand up to scrutiny; while others simply take it as a meditation on the fact that every generation will approach accepted traditions with its own set of questions.

To me, Thomas is something of a personal hero, and I regret the way religious history has treated his doubt as a matter of reproach. Thomas reads like a man who took the hard route of absolute honesty about his faith and his doubts, even when surrounded by a group of enthusiastic converts. I wouldn't mind betting that Jesus liked Thomas for his commitment to honesty far more than he was bothered by his scepticism.

According to Christian tradition, though, Thomas was not perpetually troubled with doubt. He took Christianity to India and there he was martyred for his faith. No one gets martyred for something they are ambivalent about.

Ascension

The last event mentioned in the Gospels is the ascension – again, an extraordinary story that defies belief. Luke tells the story twice – briefly at the end of his Gospel, and again as the opening of the Acts of the Apostles.

> In my former book, Theophilus, I wrote about all that Jesus began to do and to teach until the day he was taken up to heaven, after giving instructions through the Holy Spirit to the apostles he had chosen. After his suffering, he presented himself to them and gave many convincing proofs that he was alive. He appeared to them over a period of forty days and spoke about the kingdom of God. On one occasion, while he was eating with them, he gave them this command: 'Do not leave Jerusalem, but wait for the gift my Father promised, which you have heard me speak about. For John baptized with water, but in a few days you will be baptized with the Holy Spirit.'
>
> So when they met together, they asked him, 'Lord,

are you at this time going to restore the kingdom to Israel?'

He said to them: 'It is not for you to know the times or dates the Father has set by his own authority. But you will receive power when the Holy Spirit comes on you; and you will be my witnesses in Jerusalem, and in all Judea and Samaria, and to the ends of the earth.'

After he said this, he was taken up before their very eyes, and a cloud hid him from their sight.

They were looking intently up into the sky as he was going, when suddenly two men dressed in white stood beside them. 'Men of Galilee,' they said, 'why do you stand here looking into the sky? This same Jesus, who has been taken from you into heaven, will come back in the same way you have seen him go into heaven.'

(Acts 1:1–11)

The ascension is commemorated every year as one of the principal feasts in most Christian churches, on the Thursday of the sixth week of Easter.

There is a marvellous picture of the ascension in the stained-glass windows of King's College Chapel, Cambridge. The disciples are shown dressed in billowing sixteenth-century robes, looking up at the sky. There, protruding below a white cloud, are two pink feet, showing a quite literal inter-pretation of Jesus being taken up into heaven. In the cosmol-ogy of the time, heaven was taken to be a place above the sky, while hell was beneath the earth – an image that is entertainingly played out in the theology of the time. Calvin, for instance, in reasoning out what it meant for the bread and wine of Holy Communion to be the 'body and blood' of Christ, argued that if the bread and wine literally turned into the body and blood of Christ, then the resurrected body of Jesus, which was above the clouds in a literal heaven, would gradually disintegrate.

Theology – like all disciplines – has always been subject to change whenever great advances in knowledge have moved the boundaries of interpretation. One of the most controversial books in twentieth-century English theology was John A.T. Robinson's *Honest to God*, which laid out an account of what theology could mean in the space age. Before Galileo, said Robinson, heaven was taken to be 'up there' – in the sky. Early modern cosmology led to a revision in theological language, and God was referred to as 'out there'. But once we had landed men on the moon, 'out there' was outmoded language, and theology had to revise its language once again in order to make sense in a new era.

But while theology has to concern itself with making sense, art, music and literature have considerably more licence with allegory, and the ascension has all kinds of potential for bringing to life the idea of being lifted up, transformed or transported into another realm. Finzi's choral work, 'God Is Gone Up', paints a picture of its subject matter with the dramatic rising shape of the melody, creating an ascension image that is both uplifting and somewhat awe-inspiring. But in *After Ascension*, Katharine Tynan (1859–1931), one of the War poets, took the image of ascension as a mirror through which to view the way mothers cope with grief.

Pentecost

St Luke was arguably the best storyteller among the Gospel writers, and he went on to write a sequel to his Gospel. In the Acts of the Apostles he told what happened to the first generation of Jesus' followers after his death, and, picking up where he left off at the ascension, Luke moved quickly on to Pentecost as the event that began a new chapter in the lives of Jesus' followers as they gradually shifted from being a movement within Judaism to the beginnings of Christianity.

> When the day of Pentecost came, they were all together in one place. Suddenly a sound like the blowing of a violent wind came from heaven and filled the whole house where they were sitting. They saw what seemed to be tongues of fire that separated and came to rest on each of them. All of them were filled with the Holy Spirit and began to speak in other tongues as the Spirit enabled them.
>
> Now there were staying in Jerusalem God-fearing Jews from every nation under heaven. When they heard this sound, a crowd came together in bewilderment, because each one heard their own language being spoken.
>
> (Acts 2:1–6)

Pentecost has been given an assortment of interpretations during the history of the Church. Many have regarded the miraculous acquisition of other languages as a one-off event to herald the new Christian era, and some have regarded it as a metaphorical reversal of the confusion of language at the Tower of Babel (Gen. 11). Still others, especially in twentieth-century Pentecostalism, have made a connection between the coming of the Holy Spirit at Pentecost and the gifts of the Spirit that Paul wrote about later – including 'speaking in tongues', or glossolalia, which, rather than being a supernatural ability to speak foreign languages, was a mystical prayer language that St Paul called 'tongues of angels' (1 Cor. 14).

One of the oldest-known invocations of the Holy Spirit is *Veni, Creator Spiritus*, attributed to Rabanus Maurus (776–856). It is still widely used as a Christian hymn, sung at Pentecost and at various times when people or places are dedicated to God. It is usually sung to a Gregorian chant, and has been used as the basis for many later compositions, such as Maurice Duruflé's *Prelude, Adagio, and Chorale Variations on 'Veni, Creator Spiritus'*.

The fire of the Spirit was a central image for twelfth-century German abbess, mystic, poet and composer Hildegard of Bingen (1098–1179). She was interested in growing and using medicinal plants, and in one of her songs, '*O ignis Spiritus Paracliti*' ('O, Fire of the Holy Spirit'), she describes the Holy Spirit as a fire that is soothing and sweet to the taste, that cleans wounds and is an ointment for healing. Hildegard believed that God invested his Spirit into every part of creation, in the sense that every part of the natural world depends on God for its existence, and that it was the purpose of the human race to bring glory to God through caring for creation. Her concern with ecology is partly what has led to a recent revival of interest in her work.

Pentecost has similarly had quite varied portrayals in art.

Giotto (*Pentecost*, c. 1305, Scrovegni Chapel, Padua) and
Duccio di Buoninsegna (*Pentecost*, 1308, Museo dell'Opera
del Duomo, Siena) had at their disposal a style that mixed
icon with geometry to give a measured and dignified
portrayal of the reception of the Holy Spirit. But later paintings show the disciples in an excited state while little flames
floating above their heads are just close enough to realism
to look faintly ridiculous. Artists and liturgists alike have
discovered that an attempt to portray the event can end in
domesticating rather than dramatising it, making it look
more like a gas advertisement than a mystical event, and
poet and liturgist Cheryl Lawrie's poem 'Come to Think of
It . . .' is both powerful and witty in pointing out that while
Pentecost is supposed to herald a dramatic connection
between heaven and earth, its power is often lost in the
difficulties of visual representation, and the reality of the
experience is often despite, rather than because of, attempts
to capture it in word and image:

> actually, your spirit is not really like a flickering
> candle sitting on the altar, which we've protected
> from scorching with a heat proof mat
> *you burn with irrepressible, ferocious passion.*
>
> in truth, your spirit has little in common with the
> gentle breeze from the fan fluttering the orders of
> service as it rotates from the front pews during the
> children's talk
> *we can barely stand upright in the face of your love.*

luckily, your spirit barely resembles a helium filled
red balloon, rising, just out of reach, to taunt us as it
rests against the church ceiling
you would subsume us in the unrelenting hold of your
peace.

we think we have you nailed
in our fire resistant,
cyclone-proof,
red cloth swathed metaphors
thank god our inadequacy defining you has never
stopped you yet.[6]

10
Blinded by the light

There are twenty-seven books in the New Testament, and twenty-one of them are letters written by the founders of the early Christian communities to their followers and protégés, advising them on the development of Christian belief, how to manage their communities and their worship, and how to live out their new-found faith within society at large. Some of the letters were written by St Paul, and are the source of phrases like 'a thorn in my side', 'all things to all men', 'through a glass, darkly', and 'absent in body, present in spirit'.

Biographical details about St Paul appear both in his own letters and in the Acts of the Apostles, and from these we know that he was previously called Saul and was a Jewish teacher and a fierce opponent and persecutor of the Jesus movement. But then he had the original 'Damascus Road experience', did a complete about-turn in his views and eventually became so significant in the establishment of the early Christian communities that many scholars believe without his influence Christianity might never have taken root and become a religion in its own right.

Saul was still breathing out murderous threats against the Lord's disciples. He went to the high priest and asked him for letters to the synagogues in Damascus, so that if he found any there who belonged to the Way, whether men or women, he might take them as prisoners to Jerusalem. As he neared Damascus on his journey, suddenly a light from heaven flashed around him. He fell to the ground and heard a voice say to him, 'Saul, Saul, why do you persecute me?'

'Who are you, Lord?' Saul asked.

'I am Jesus, whom you are persecuting,' he replied. 'Now get up and go into the city, and you will be told what you must do.'

The men travelling with Saul stood there speechless; they heard the sound but did not see anyone. Saul got up from the ground, but when he opened his eyes he could see nothing. So they led him by the hand into Damascus. For three days he was blind, and did not eat or drink anything.

(Acts 9:1–9)

A 'Damascus Road experience' is a complete about-turn in attitude or belief, but another phrase that derives from the same story means quite the opposite. 'Blinded by the light' usually means that being too close to something blinds you to the truth. Bruce Springsteen used the phrase for a song, later covered by Manfred Mann, about how falling in love can have the same effect.

Love is all you need

By virtue of the fact that it is still the most popular reading at weddings, one of the most famous pieces of St Paul's writing is his hymn to love.

> Love is patient, love is kind. It does not envy, it does not boast, it is not proud. It does not dishonour others, it is not self-seeking, it is not easily angered, it keeps no record of wrongs. Love does not delight in evil but rejoices with the truth. It always protects, always trusts, always hopes, always perseveres.
>
> Love never fails. But where there are prophecies, they will cease; where there are tongues, they will be stilled; where there is knowledge, it will pass away. For we know in part and we prophesy in part, but when completeness comes, what is in part disappears. When I was a child, I talked like a child, I thought like a child, I reasoned like a child. When I became a man, I put the ways of childhood behind me. For now we see only a reflection as in a mirror; then we shall see face to face. Now I know in part; then I shall know fully, even as I am fully known.
>
> And now these three remain: faith, hope and love. But the greatest of these is love.
>
> (1 Cor. 13:4–13)

Elizabeth Barrett Browning, in her famous Sonnet XLIII, 'How Do I Love Thee', borrowed another New Testament phrase to describe her love for Robert Browning:

> I love thee to the depth and breadth and height
> My soul can reach.[1]

She was writing not only about the intense feelings of falling in love, but about the way in which loving someone else transforms the lover – something that she knew more about than most. Barrett Browning had spent her early life caged in both by physical illness and by a bullying and controlling father and, incapable of finding any escape, she passed much of her time lying on a day-bed. It was the reckless, over-whelming quality of her love for Robert that gave her the strength to overcome her *ennui*, escape her diminished existence and flee with him to Italy. Once she discovered the capacity to love Robert as much as she loved herself, the frail, pale and tragic girl was transformed into a passionate, energetic and creative woman.

It is no mistake, then, that Barrett Browning drew on biblical phraseology to describe her love which, like the love described by the New Testament writers, would not evaporate in the light of day. 'I am convinced,' wrote St Paul, 'that neither death nor life . . . neither height nor depth, nor anything else in all creation, will be able to separate us from the love of God that is in Christ Jesus our Lord' (Rom. 8:38–9). Later another author wrote to the church of Ephesus that he wanted them 'to grasp how wide and long and high and deep is the love of Christ' (Eph. 3:17–18).

'Love never fails' is a great sentiment for a wedding, of course, but although reams of poetry and music are inspired by the glories of love, there is just as much written about the agony of heartbreak. From the twelfth-century troubadours to Neil Finn or Paul Simon, some of the best music in the world has been inspired by love falling apart. So why was St Paul so convinced that love could prove invincible?

The clue to his certainty is hidden in the original script, which was written in a dialect of Greek known as *Koiné*. Whereas in English we use one word to describe many different kinds of love – love for our country, for our children, for our friends, and romantic love – the Greeks were very precise in their description of love. They had four different words to define different kinds of love that interact and cross over with each other.

Philia describes a bond of love between friends, nurtured through sharing a common interest. *Storge* means affection, or fondness through familiarity – the kind of love that grows over time between neighbours or colleagues with whom you have little in common, but whom you have known for years and grown to care about. *Eros* is what we would describe as romance, or falling 'in love'. It describes that deeply infatuated state with another person which tends to make one overlook faults or difficulties and become completely wrapped up in the other.

But when St Paul writes of the love that never fails, he does not use any of these words. He employs a fourth word, *agape*, which is a pure, committed and completely selfless love, always concerned with the other. You are not at the mercy of feelings with *agape* love – rather than a feeling that overwhelms you, it is a commitment to act in love towards the other, regardless of the circumstances. This is the love that never fails.

St Paul, then, was writing not about romance, but about another kind of love altogether. But since his words are read regularly at weddings, it is worth noting that the Bible does not imply that we have to choose between different kinds of love, but that the enduring quality of *agape* love is the foundation of all the rest. Romantic love is unreliable and might evaporate overnight, but it finds its reply in the come-what-may commitment of *agape* which – according to St Paul, at least – is the definition of God.

Heaven and hell

If the Bible begins with the dawn of time, then perhaps it ought to close with the end of everything, whatever that might mean. The closing pages of the Bible certainly speak of the 'Alpha and Omega', 'the beginning and the end', and 'a new heaven and a new earth'. But it is surprising to discover that there is quite a bit of variation in the Bible when it comes to expectations of heaven, hell or the afterlife.

The Psalms often mention Sheol, which is supposed to be a place where the dead sleep under the earth and cannot feel or know anything. Various passages in the prophets and the book of Revelation include descriptions that seem to be a glimpse into the afterlife, but even here some of it is more suggestive of a better future here on earth than a place in the blue yonder.

The idea of heaven and hell, along with purgatory and limbo, crops up all over the place in literature, from Dante's *Divine Comedy* to Dickens's *A Christmas Carol*. But Christian belief about these ideas has followed the surrounding culture as much as it has influenced it. Christian tradition has, at different times, included ideas such as hell as a place of fire and endless torment, purgatory as a kind of post-death penitentiary, limbo, demons or evil spirits who were once rebel angels, and Satan, the enemy of God and the chief evil spirit.

Hell

The 'harrowing of hell' was a major theme in medieval art and literature, and appears in most mystery play cycles. It derives from the Apostles' Creed, where it says that after Jesus died and before his resurrection, 'he descended into hell'. Quite what that means has been a matter of some controversy, but a belief grew up that when Jesus died he went down into the underworld to rescue from limbo people who had died before him, so that his salvation would be effective for them as well as for the living. A painting by Spanish artist Bartolomeo Bertejo, *Christ Leads the Patriarchs from Hell to Paradise* (c. 1480), shows a procession of biblical characters following Jesus out of hell, led by Adam and Eve, followed by Solomon, the Queen of Sheba and Methuselah, who was Noah's grandfather and – reportedly dying at the age of 969 – the oldest man in the Bible.

Shakespeare's *Hamlet* oscillates between conflicting Catholic and Protestant beliefs about the afterlife. The Protestant reformers had abandoned the idea of purgatory and believed that upon death a person's soul would go directly to heaven or hell. When the ghostly figure of Hamlet's father appears, the play reflects both Catholic acceptance of a ghost returning from purgatory and Protestant belief that ghosts are from the devil. This ghost, though, claimed that he was suffering the torment of purgatory because he had been murdered before he had the chance to be absolved of his sins:

> Doom'd for a certain term to walk the night,
> And for the day confin'd to fast in fires,
> Till the foul crimes done in my days of nature
> Are burnt and purged away. But that I am forbid
> To tell the secrets of my prison-house,
> I could a tale unfold whose lightest word
> Would harrow up thy soul, freeze thy young blood,
> Make thy two eyes like stars start from their spheres,
> Thy knotted and combined locks to part
> And each particular hair to stand on end,
> Like quills upon the fretful porpentine.[2]

'To be or not to be . . .' is one of the most famous speeches in English literature, where Hamlet contemplates the relative merits of being alive or dead. But his real dilemma was an unresolved anxiety in Elizabethan England – the question as to whether suicide would automatically lead to eternal damnation. There was a cruel logic to this idea. Although suicide was not specifically forbidden in the Ten Commandments, it was treated as being against the sixth commandment, 'Thou shalt not kill.' According to Roman Catholic doctrine murder was a mortal sin which, because it was committed deliberately, could only be forgiven through confession and absolution. But clearly, if a person commits suicide, they are then not able to make confession, and therefore suicide would automatically lead to damnation. Hamlet is given pause, then, by:

The dread of something after death,
The undiscovered country from whose bourn
No traveller returns, puzzles the will
And makes us rather bear those ills we have
Than fly to others that we know not of.

Samuel Taylor Coleridge, as a young radical, was adamantly opposed to the idea that life on earth should be subsumed under the goal of life after death, and later one of his disciples, F.D. Maurice, got into serious hot water for developing this idea further. Maurice was a professor at King's College, London, when he published *Theological Essays* in 1853. In it he suggested that there was no such thing as eternal punishment in fiery flames, only a choice between aligning oneself with God as the source of love, grace and goodness, and refusing God. His rejection of eternal punishment was partly to do with his belief that the doctrine had as much to do with social control as it did with theology. Similar ideas were picked up by other writers, including C.S. Lewis in his novel *The Great Divorce* (1945), and eventually in the 1990s the Church of England caught up with Maurice and clarified their doctrine along similar lines. But although F.D. Maurice turned out to be a prophet before his time, in 1853 his move towards a kinder theology was not welcomed. His superiors regarded his views as heretical, dangerous and likely to unsettle the minds of the students, and they sacked him from his job.

Heaven

The final book of the Bible is a mystical book called Revelation (sometimes called the Apocalypse of John, or the Revelation of St John the Divine). In it St John recalls some visions he had while in exile on the island of Patmos, beginning when Jesus stood before him, 'dressed in a robe reaching down to his feet and with a golden sash around his chest. The hair on his head was white like wool, as white as snow, and his eyes were like blazing fire' (Rev. 1:13–14). After a series of warnings to his readers about being faithful to Christ, John then says that before him was a 'door standing open in heaven' through which John was able to see what heaven was like, and something of what the future held.

In places John's account reads like fantasy literature, with characters that easily rival those in *Dr Who* or *Lord of the Rings*. John's mythical creatures include the four horsemen, the whore of Babylon and a dragon who is often taken to be an embodiment of the devil himself. There are assorted cherubs and angels, hundreds of people dressed in clothes of purest white, and some creatures that are part human, part animal, with several pairs of wings and eyes all over their bodies. Unfortunately for the modern reader, much of Revelation is almost incomprehensible, but there are passages where at least the basic gist is clear. The visions are meant to give messages of warning against evil, predicting judgement for those who are evil and the promise of a bright and secure future for those who are good. One of the features of the paradise John saw was that 'there will be no more sea'. To beach lovers this may not sound like heaven at all, but the sea was seen as symbolic of darkness and chaos, the home of sea monsters who represented evil. Revelation culminates in a vision of a world in which (in the language of St John) the light will at last overcome the darkness:

> Then I saw 'a new heaven and a new earth,' for the first heaven and the first earth had passed away, and there was no longer any sea. I saw the Holy City, the new Jerusalem, coming down out of heaven from God, prepared as a bride beautifully dressed for her husband. And I heard a loud voice from the throne saying, 'Look! God's dwelling place is now among the people, and he will dwell with them. They will be his people, and God himself will be with them and be their God. "He will wipe every tear from their eyes. There will be no more death" or mourning or crying or pain, for the old order of things has passed away.'
>
> He who was seated on the throne said, 'I am making everything new!' Then he said, 'Write this down, for these words are trustworthy and true.'
>
> He said to me: 'It is done. I am the Alpha and the Omega, the Beginning and the End. To the thirsty I will give water without cost from the spring of the water of life.'
>
> (Rev. 21:1–6)

Many believe that John's book was written in a deliberately obscure form so that those who understood his symbolism would get the message, without the letter itself creating a threat to their safety. Revelation could have been a veiled warning about coming persecutions and political unrest, and it was also a promise that keeping the faith would turn out right in the end. But over time, some of his visions became associated less with a call to imagine a better world into being, and more with a heaven that existed in another dimension – a place to which people would go after they died, a place of peace, joy and plenitude, populated with those who love God, where at last they would be free of persecution and danger (bear in mind, of course, that this was written to the early Christians, who were literally thrown to the lions or crucified for their faith).

Jerusalem

The song 'Jerusalem' has been described as England's unofficial national anthem. It is a popular wedding hymn, was adopted by the England cricket team as their theme song (and less fortunately by the British National Party), and by tradition is sung as the penultimate item in a series of patriotic pieces at the Last Night of the Proms – the closing night of an annual summer series of concerts in London. The status of 'Jerusalem' as a patriotic hymn dates back to its publication in 1926, after which it quickly found its place in school song books and college choir repertoires of the 1920s and 1930s, but it has its origins, perhaps surprisingly, in the Women's Institute. Do not let the cosy image of cakes and jam deceive you, however, for both the WI and 'Jerusalem' have their roots in lawless protest.

The words of 'Jerusalem' were originally the preface to William Blake's poem *Milton* (1804–10), which was inspired by *Paradise Lost* (1667). In it Blake relates how Adam's disobedience in the garden of Eden led to the devastation of paradise and a life of toil and struggle, but he departs from Milton's own views in a number of places. Although he loved *Paradise Lost*, Blake found Milton's God too distant and judgemental and his view of humanity too harsh. Christian thought has always included the idea that men and women are made in the image of God, but there are different schools of thought within Christianity as to how much that image-of-God-ness was wiped out by the effects of sin. Some theologians put so much emphasis on the devastation of sin that they almost seemed to suggest that salvation was a matter of starting again from scratch. Others reminded their readers that despite humanity's flaws they were still made in the image of God, and salvation was a matter of restoration. Blake, however, in seeking to bring a corrective to Milton's harsh views, went far beyond a positive and hopeful view of humanity to give them a semi-divine quality.

Blake's 'Jerusalem', then, is an interesting blend of Christianity and paganism. It starts with the apocryphal story that as a young man Jesus visited England with Joseph of Arimathea, a man who appears in the Gospels to provide a tomb for Jesus and who, according to tradition, was a tin merchant. Blake imagines Christ standing on the rolling hills, blessing all that he sees. Blake's vision of a peaceful, pastoral Christian England is interrupted by the ugly reality of the 'dark satanic mills', which have been given various interpretations ranging from the factories of industrialised England, to the corrupt institutions of parliament and the Church of England, to the amassing of munitions in London in 1893 when the threat of war with France escalated.[3] Blake then goes on to contrast the machinery of war with 'mental fight' – the weapon of the imagination, and his belief in the power of ideas to bring social change.

Blake's words were clearly the seeds of peaceful revolution, but when they were set to music more than a century later, it was as a protest song for another kind of social change altogether. In the latter quarter of the nineteenth century, the vote was given for the first time to ordinary working men, but women were not included. A campaign of protest was begun by a woman named Millicent Fawcett, and by the early twentieth century the movement for women's suffrage was hitting the headlines on a regular basis. The suffragettes began with peaceful, non-violent protest, but after some years of being consistently ignored, they began breaking windows and starting fires in an effort to bring attention to their quest for the right to vote. And to keep up their morale, the suffragettes always set out on their protests singing rallying songs.

When war broke out in 1914, their acts of civil disobedience were halted and women pitched in with the war effort by working in the fields and factories. But they continued their campaign in vocal and peaceful ways through meetings and rallies. Then in 1916, the sixteen-line preface of Blake's 1804 epic *Milton: A Poem* was reproduced in a volume of patriotic poetry. These were sent to the English composer Hubert Parry, whose wife was a suffragette, and he set them to music for a 1916 rally of the 'Fight for the Right' movement in London's Queen's Hall. The tune caught the imagination of Millicent Fawcett, and she wrote to Hubert Parry telling him that it should become the women voters' hymn.

After the war ended in 1918, the vote was granted to

women over thirty, and Parry himself conducted his hymn at a concert to mark the final stage in the Votes for Women Campaign. It was after this concert that the hymn was given the name 'Jerusalem' and was adopted as the anthem of the Women's Institute. Another decade passed before the Equal Franchise Act was passed in 1928 granting the vote to women over twenty-one, so it was not until the 1929 general election that women voted on an equal footing with men.

While Parry had written a great melody for 'Jerusalem', the musical arrangement was rather pedestrian, and after his death in 1918 the song might easily have got lost in the mists of time. But what really gave it wings to fly was the brilliance of Edward Elgar's orchestration. Elgar had the musical capacity to write a stadium anthem, and he added an orchestral score to Parry's tune in time for the Leeds Festival of 1922, after which it quickly became a popular national hymn, was adopted for the Last Night of the Proms, and began to be sung in schools and chapels up and down the land. So it was that in the inter-war years it gathered layers of patriotic meaning as Britain recovered from the First World War.

Considering its origins – a damning indictment of England as a kind of hell on earth – it is somewhat ironic that 'Jerusalem' ended up as a patriotic hymn, celebrating establishment rather than revolution. But despite Blake's strange mix of fantasy and biblical imagery, 'Jerusalem' does capture something of the essence of the New Testament idea of heaven. They both put forward a vision of a better world, and rather than passively waiting for God to act, they both express a fierce determination to see the human race actively involved in bringing that vision into reality through the power of the imagination, infused with the love and goodness of God.

You might expect that a biblical account of heaven would resemble something like a return to the paradise of the garden of Eden, as described in Genesis. But heaven is poetically described in Revelation not as the garden paradise of Eden, but as an idealised version of Jerusalem – an immense tree-lined city built around a crystal-clear, life-giving river, with no need for religion, as God's presence would be everywhere, filling the city with light.

But although there is a vision of heaven, the closing pages of the Bible are not focused entirely on a heaven in the blue yonder. They are just as much concerned with a new earth, a new era of peace and justice right here on the earth we inhabit. The Christian view of the future, then, is not all pie-in-the-sky in another dimension beyond this world. It is a much more revolutionary idea of a transformed world. Heaven, according to the Bible, begins here on earth.

A few suggestions for further reading

Armstrong, Karen, *The Bible: The Biography* (Atlantic Books, 2008).

Atwan, R. and L. Wieder (eds), *Chapters into Verse* (Oxford University Press, 2000).

Cohn, Norman, *Noah's Flood: Genesis Story in Western Thought* (Yale University Press, 1996).

Dyas, Dee and Esther Hughes, *The Bible in Western Culture* (Routledge, 2005).

Nicolson, Adam, *Power and Glory* (HarperCollins, 2003).

Jasper, David and Stephen Prickett, *The Bible and Literature, A Reader* (Blackwell, 1999).

Finkel, I.L. and M.J. Seymour (eds), *Babylon* (British Museum Press, 2008).

Ward, Keith, *The Word of God* (SPCK, 2010).

Notes

Bible Translations

Preface

1   Samuel Taylor Coleridge, *Table Talk*, 14 June 1830.
    (J. Murray, 1836), p.76.

Chapter 1

1   Various scholars have tried to identify the original accounts, and although it is impossible to recreate the editing process, it does help to make sense of why conflicting accounts of similar stories appear side by side in the Bible.

2   John Polkinghorne, *The Times*, 19 September 2008.

3   Augustine, *De Genesi ad Litteram*, Book II (my translation).

4   John Milton *Paradise Lost*, 1667, Book VII, 205–8, 13–16.

5   Gerard Manley Hopkins, 'God's Grandeur', from *Poems* (Humphrey Milford, 1918).

6   Whenever the word 'LORD' appears in capitals in English-language Bibles, it represents a translation of YHWH, a four-letter code that indicates the name of the Hebrew God known as the tetragrammaton. By Jewish tradition the name of God was considered so holy that it could not be spoken aloud. Where it has been given pronunciation it was previously translated as Jehovah, but is nowadays usually given as Yahweh.

7   S. Todd, 'Models and Menstruation: *Spare Rib* Magazine, Feminism, Femininity and Pleasure', www.sussex.ac.uk/Units/SPT/journal/pdf/issue1-5.pdf (March 2003); M. Rowe, '*Spare Rib* Magazine and its Relationship to the Women's Movement', in *Women and the Media Conference Report* (1974).

8   Peter Redgrove, 'Intimate Supper', in M. Roberts (ed.), *The Faber Book of Modern Verse*, 4th ed. (Faber and Faber, 1982), p. 399.

Chapter 2

1   Chaucer, 'Nun's Priest's Tale', lines 421–4.

2   V.A. Kolve points out that the 'Cook's Tale' is also

reminiscent of the parable of the prodigal son, in
*Chaucer and the Imagery of Narrative: The First Five
Canterbury Tales* (Stanford University Press, 1984),
p. 276.

3   David Hume, *The History of England*, vol. I, ch. xvii,
(Phillips Sampson & co., 1856).

4   The person from Porlock has in turn become something
of a figure of speech for mundane or inexplicable
reasons for delay. Roger McGough commented in one of
his own poems that he believed Coleridge 'got stuck',
and Douglas Adams parodies Coleridge's tale in *Dirk
Gently's Holistic Detective Agency* by making the visitor
from Porlock a time traveller who deliberately prevented
Coleridge from finishing the poem in order to save the
human race.

5   Daniel Lanois, Acadie (Opal Records, 1989).

6   *Hamlet*, Act 3, Scene iii, lines 40–1.

7   Jonathan Swift, *Polite Conversation*, no. 214 (1738).

8   John Steinbeck, *East of Eden* (first published 1952;
Penguin Classics ed. 2000), ch. 24, p. 301.

9   John Steinbeck, *Journal of a Novel: The* East of Eden
Letters (The Viking Press, Inc., 1969; Penguin Books,
1990).

10 *The Epic of Gilgamesh*, trans. Andrew George (Penguin
Classics, 2003).

Chapter 3

1   There are founding mothers too, although with a few
notable exceptions the Bible record is written with a bias
towards its patriarchs. This has become an issue of
unresolved debate in churches, where the Bible is treated
not only as a collection of ancient stories, but as Holy

Scripture which influences how people structure their lives now. It is certainly possible to read the narratives of the Old Testament with an eye to the way that the women influenced events, and recent decades have seen some excellent theological work on how to read the Bible with an inclusive agenda – both by recognising the fact that, against the odds, women did feature strongly in stories from a patriarchal society, and also by challenging the sexist assumptions of much of the Bible's narratives. All the same, it would be disingenuous in any context to pretend that the Bible is not patriarchal: for the most part it was written by men, and about men, in societies where the rights of women were given very little attention.

2   Giorgio Vasari, *Lives of the Artists*, trans. J.C. and P. Bondanella (Oxford World Classics, 1991), p. 87.

3   Wilfred Owen, 'The Parable of the Old Men and the Young', in *The Works of Wilfred Owen* (Wordsworth, 1994).

Chapter 4

1   The monastery, which houses a large number of important ancient documents and manuscripts, was named after St Catherine, who was martyred by being tied to a wheel and burned – this is the gruesome origin of the name for the 'Catherine wheel' firework.

2   William Faulkner, *Go Down Moses and Other Stories* (Random House, 1942).

Chapter 5

1   Jeff Buckley, 'Grace', © Sony Music, 1994.

2   Handel's *Messiah* also uses Coverdale's translation in several places, in preference to the King James Version.

Chapter 6

1   Elijah's life is recorded in 1 and 2 Kings.
2   Steve Earle, *Jerusalem* (Epic Records, 2002).
3   Henk Van Os, Netherlands Art, 1400–1600 (Yale University Press, 2000), p. 72.
4   Codex Vyssengradensis, Czech National Library, Prague.
5   Macclesfield Psalter, Folio 9, Fitzwilliam Museum, Cambridge.
6   From Siegfried Sassoon, *Counter-Attack and Other Poems* (E.P. Dutton, 1918).

Chapter 8

1   Noel Rowe, 'Magnificat', in *Next to Nothing* (Vagabond Press, 2004).
2   *Australian eJournal of Theology*, Issue 5, August 2005.
3   John Milton, 'On the Morning of Christ's Nativity' (1629).
4   U.A. Fanthorpe, 'BC:AD', Christmas Poems (Enitharman Press, 2002), p. 23.
5   Shakespeare, *Hamlet*, Act 1, Scene i, lines 158–64.
6   T.H. White, *The Once and Future King*, Book 2, (Collins, 1958), p. 248.
7   The complete Bible was printed and published in English for the first time in 1535, the work of Miles Coverdale, who drew heavily on William Tyndale's 1525 English New Testament as well as Luther's German translation and Erasmus's Latin. Later Coverdale was also involved in producing The Great Bible (1539–41), the Geneva Bible (1560) and the Bishops Bible (1568), which is often regarded as a rough draft of the King James Version.
8   This was an adaptation of the seventeenth-century Scottish tune 'Gilderoy'.

9   William Langland, Piers Plowman. Passus, 17, 18.

10   Henri Nouwen, *The Return of the Prodigal Son, A Story of Homecoming* (Darton, Longman and Todd, 1992).

11   Frank Cottrell Boyce, *Millions* (Macmillan, 2004), p. 174.

12   Julian of Norwich, *Revelation of Divine Love*, transl. M. L. Del Mastro (Liguori Publications, 1994), pp. 191–2.

13   Joni Mitchell, 'Magdalene Laundries', © Crazy Cow Music, 1994.

Chapter 9

1   Judas Arthur Quiller-Couch (ed.), *The Oxford Book of Ballads* (1910).

2   Barbara C. Raw, *The Art and Background of Old English Poetry* (London, 1978), p. 82.

3   Jonathan Sacks, in *The Times* (date unknown).

4   Samuel Taylor Coleridge, *Confessions of an Inquiring Spirit,* (Edward Moxon & Co. 1863), p. 47.

5   Samuel Taylor Coleridge, Aids to Reflection, 17th Edition (Edward Moxon & Co., 1867), p. 75.

6   Cheryl Lawrie, *Hold This Space* (Proost, 2008), used with permission.

Chapter 10

1   Elizabeth Barrett Browning, Sonnet 43, cf. Ephesians 3:18 (Ephesians is attributed to St Paul, but was almost certainly written by someone else, after Paul's death).

2   Shakespeare, *Hamlet*, Act 1, Scene v, lines 10–20.

3   D. Erdman, *Blake: Prophet against Empire*, 3rd ed. (Dover Publications, 1991).

Index